Sequencing

Grade 5

by
Claire Norman

Published by Instructional Fair
an imprint of
Frank Schaffer Publications®

Sequencing - Grade 5

Table of Contents

Author: Claire Norman
Editor: Lisa Hancock
Cover Artist: Cindy Cutler
Interior Artist: Don Ellens

Frank Schaffer Publications®

Instructional Fair is an imprint of Frank Schaffer Publications.

Send all inquiries to:
Frank Schaffer Publications
8720 Orion Place
Columbus, OH 43240-2111

Sequencing—Grade 5

ISBN 0-88012-965-4

7 8 9 10 11 QPD 11 10 09 08

Being Prepared

Name ______________________________

Write **first, second, third** and **fourth** in front of each set of sentences to show their correct order. Rewrite them in that order in a paragraph.

________ The students lined up just as Miss Jones had instructed.

________ They came back into the building, and the principal announced they had emptied the school in less than one minute.

________ Miss Jones, the 5th grade teacher, informed her students what to do in case of a fire drill.

________ The fire alarm sounded during social studies.

________ He jumped out of bed and hurriedly washed and dressed in the clothes he had laid out the night before.

________ Bob's alarm went off at 5:00 a.m. Saturday morning.

________ Bob grabbed his pack and went out to join the troop for an all-day expedition in the mountains.

________ The scout leader pulled up in front of Bob's house just as he finished a light breakfast.

• Draw what comes next.

In the Forties

Name ____________________________

Write **first, second, third** and **fourth** in front of each set of sentences to show their correct order. Rewrite them in that order in a paragraph in the spaces below.

_________ The Senate voted unanimously to declare war, and the House of Representatives had one dissenting vote.

_________ On Sunday morning, December 7, 1941, Japanese bombers attacked the United States naval base at Pearl Harbor.

_________ He asked them to declare war on Japan.

_________ On Monday, President Roosevelt appeared before a special joint session of Congress.

_________ President Roosevelt was vacationing when he suffered a stroke and died.

_________ His Vice President, Harry Truman, was sworn in as President and had to assume the office while the nation was still at war.

_________ Truman made the decision to drop the atomic bomb on Japan.

_________ The Japanese formally surrendered aboard the S.S. Missouri in Tokyo Bay.

- Circle the tallest building in the United States.

The Chrysler Building The Sears Tower The Empire State Building

Stories in Nature

Name ______________________________

Number the pictures in order to make a story.

Write sentences that tell about the pictures in the order you numbered them.

____

____

____

____

Number these pictures also to make a story.

Write sentences that tell about the pictures in the order you numbered them.

____

____

____

____

____

- Circle the latest time.

half past 3 o'clock p.m. **3:41 p.m.** **20 minutes to 4:00 p.m.**

Skill: Organizing Pictures

Birds of a Feather

Name ______________________________

Number the pictures in order to make a story.

Write sentences that tell about the pictures in the order you numbered them.

1. ______________________________
2. ______________________________
3. ______________________________
4. ______________________________

Number these pictures also to make a story.

Write sentences that tell about the pictures in the order you numbered them.

1. ______________________________
2. ______________________________
3. ______________________________
4. ______________________________

- Circle the best buy.

49¢ each **4 for $1.95** **3 for $1.50**

Story Strips

Name ______________________________

Number the pictures in order.

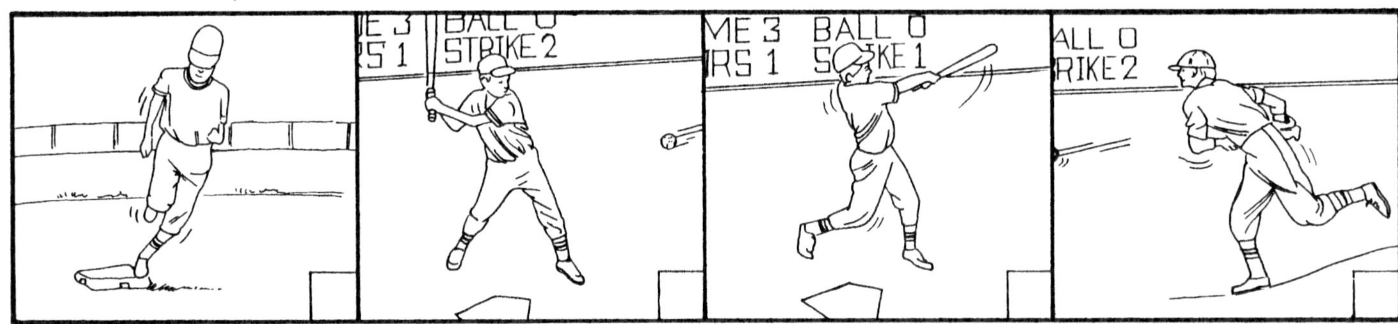

Use the pictures in order to write a story.

____

____

____

____

____

____

____

Number the pictures in order.

Use the pictures in order to write a story.

____

____

____

____

____

____

____

• Write what comes next.

concerts, concert, days, day, weeks, ______

Skill: Sequencing from Pictures

A Long Tale

Name ______________________________

Number the pictures in order to make a story.

Write a story following the order you numbered the pictures.

____

____

____

____

____

____

____

____

____

____

____

• Draw what comes next. ________

Why?

Name ______________________________

Read the following sentences. Mark an X on the line before each sentence that has a cause.

Hint: A sentence with a **cause** tells about something that happened and also tells why it happened.

____ Twelve children went on the field trip.
____ John and Jeff are scrubbing the walls where they spattered paint.
____ Bells rang for an hour to announce the end of the war.
____ We went shopping and to the movies last night.
____ The storm took off part of our roof, so we had to have a roofer come and fix it.
____ Be careful with scissors so you don't cut anyone by mistake.
____ The pigs at the farm were born late last Tuesday evening.
____ The national guard was called out to help the flood victims.
____ We played a guessing game after dinner.
____ The room was completely dark when the lights went out.
____ When the red towel was put into the washing machine by mistake, the white shirt turned pink.
____ The driver of the automobile accidentally hit the deer when it dashed across the highway.
____ Go to the store to get some paper and paste.
____ Twenty-two hospital volunteers met at my house yesterday afternoon.
____ The boys took care of their baby sister.
____ The car ran out of gas on the highway so Tom had to walk two miles to get gas.
____ Our baby sitter locked her keys in her car and she had no way of getting to our house.
____ Penny had several packages in her arms and couldn't open the door.
____ The baby was up most of the night.
____ The delivery man left two packages at our neighbor's house.

- Draw what comes next.

____

Find the Cause

Name ____________________________

Underline the part of each sentence which is the cause. A cause makes something else happen.

Examples: The smoke alarm sounds when the temperature near it rises.

Father missed his plane and was late for his appointment.

1. I fell on the sidewalk because it was icy.
2. I forgot my homework so I had to stay after school and do it.
3. The firemen had to come with their long ladder because my cat was trapped high in the tree.
4. When the full moon is out on a clear night, it seems almost like daytime.
5. Since the wind is blowing from the West, we will probably have the storm tomorrow they are having in the West today.
6. I used grandpa's typewriter to write my report, and I got an "A" for neatness.
7. When Hillary was in the hospital, she received many get-well cards.
8. The weather was so warm in December that the buds on the trees began to open.
9. If it is going to rain, the barometer will fall.
10. Because we won more games than any team in our league, we are going to the state championship finals.
11. Our lawn is torn up from the geese grazing on it every morning in winter.
12. A mouse was getting in our cupboard every night, so we set a trap.
13. If the painter comes tomorrow, we will have to get up early.
14. Jane won the spelling bee because she was the only one who knew how to spell "separate."
15. When the general came to inspect the troops, they stood at attention.

- Write what comes next.

HWQ IMQ JWQ KMQ LWQ MMQ ______

I Did It

Name ______________________________

Do as directed below.

List five things you did after school yesterday.

1. ______________________________
2. ______________________________
3. ______________________________
4. ______________________________
5. ______________________________

Write five things you did before you came to school this morning.

1. ______________________________
2. ______________________________
3. ______________________________
4. ______________________________
5. ______________________________

Write five things you did last weekend.

1. ______________________________
2. ______________________________
3. ______________________________
4. ______________________________
5. ______________________________

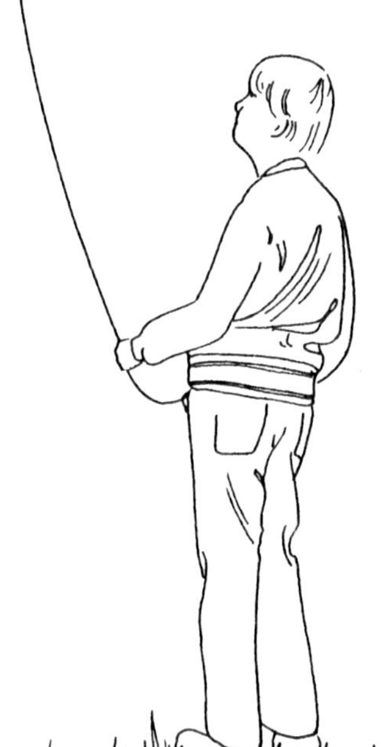

Choose one thing you did from the lists above.
Write about the one you chose. Tell what you did in the order in which you did it.

1. ______________________________
2. ______________________________
3. ______________________________
4. ______________________________
5. ______________________________

• Write what comes next.

1 3 6 10 15 ______

Skill: Sequencing from Directions

Going Straight

Name ______________________________

Follow the directions in each section. You will need a ruler and a pencil.

Start at the dot. Draw a 3 inch line from it directly to the right. From the end of that line, draw a 1½ inch line straight down. Connect the end of the second line with the beginning of the first line.

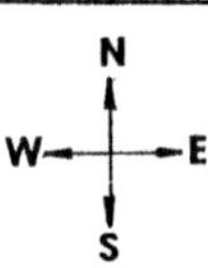

Begin at the dot and draw 1 inch lines in all four directions. Connect the tip of the north line with the tip of the east line. Connect the tip of the west line with the tip of the south line.

Begin at the ●. Draw a 1½-inch line from it directly to the right. From the end of that line draw a line to the ▲. From the▲ draw a 1-inch line directly to the left. From that line draw a 2-inch line straight down. From the end of that line draw a 3-inch line directly to the right. From the end of that line draw a 2½-inch line straight up. From the end of that line draw a line to the ■, then to the △, next to the ○, the ✱, the □ and last to the ☆. From there draw a 2-inch line down.

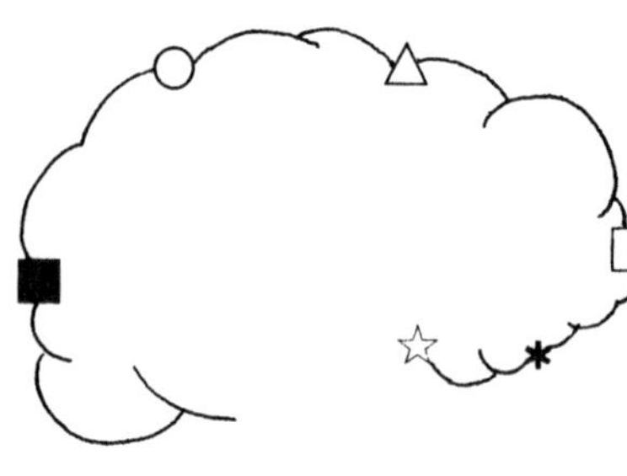

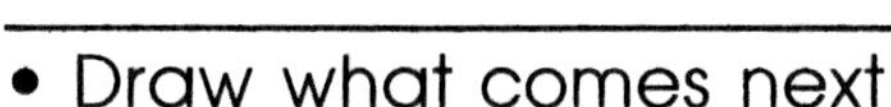

• Draw what comes next.

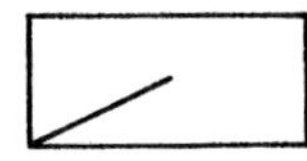
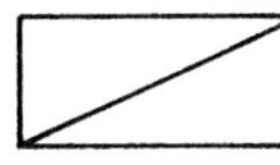
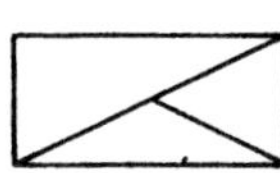
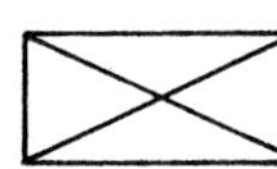

____

From John's House to Jerry's

Name ______________________________

There are several ways to get from John's house to Jerry's. Mark the route you would take on the map.

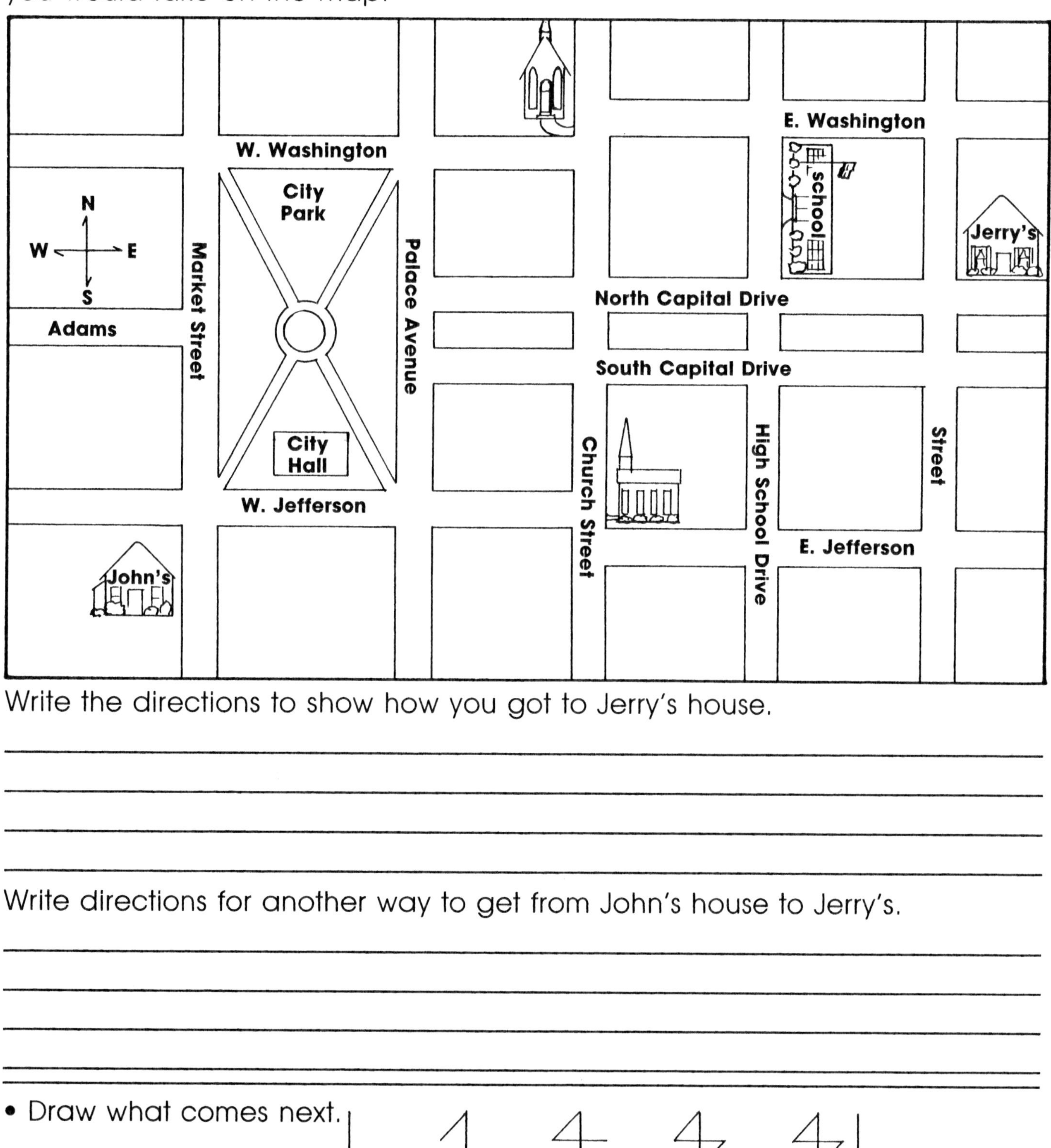

Write the directions to show how you got to Jerry's house.

____

____

____

____

Write directions for another way to get from John's house to Jerry's.

____

____

____

____

- Draw what comes next.

Hot Biscuits

Name ______________________________

Number the recipe in order so it is possible to make twelve delicious biscuits.

____ Bake until golden brown, about 12 minutes.

____ Add 6 tablespoons of shortening to the flour mixture.

____ Preheat the oven to 450° after gathering and measuring the ingredients.

____ Remove from the oven.

____ Set out the necessary utensils and ingredients.

____ Cut the shortening into the flour mixture with a knife until the mixture is crumbly.

____ Measure out the amounts of various ingredients that you will be combining.

____ Loosen the biscuits from the baking sheet with a spatula and put them on a serving dish.

____ Mix 2 cups flour, 2½ teaspoons baking powder and 1 teaspoon salt in a mixing bowl.

____ Pour in 1 cup of cold milk and stir until blended.

____ Serve while hot.

____ Drop heaping tablespoons of dough 2 inches apart onto a baking sheet.

____ Place baking sheet in oven.

List the ingredients and utensils needed for this recipe.

Ingredients	Utensils
______________________	______________________
______________________	______________________
______________________	______________________
______________________	______________________
______________________	______________________

• Circle the widest angle.

Make an Airplane

Name ____________________

Order the illustrated instructions below by writing a number below each box.

First cut out the cockpit on three sides in the center of the box and fold it back to make a windshield.

___

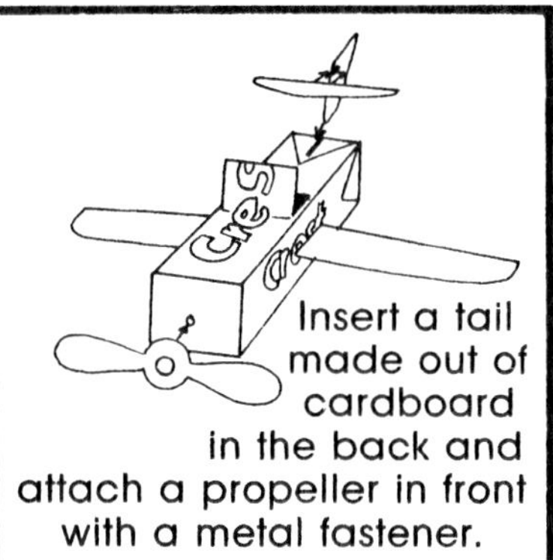

Insert a tail made out of cardboard in the back and attach a propeller in front with a metal fastener.

___

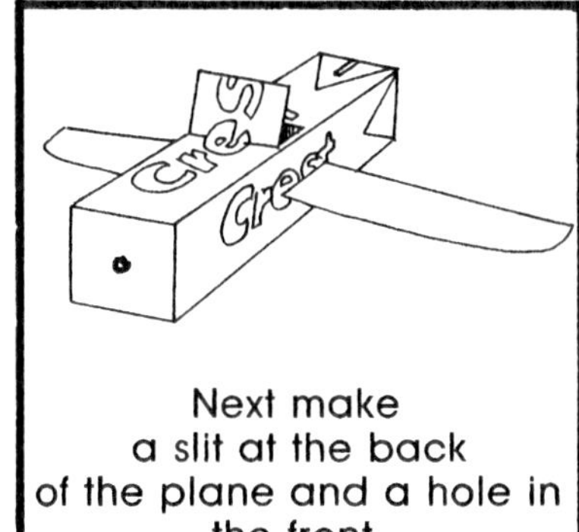

Next make a slit at the back of the plane and a hole in the front.

___

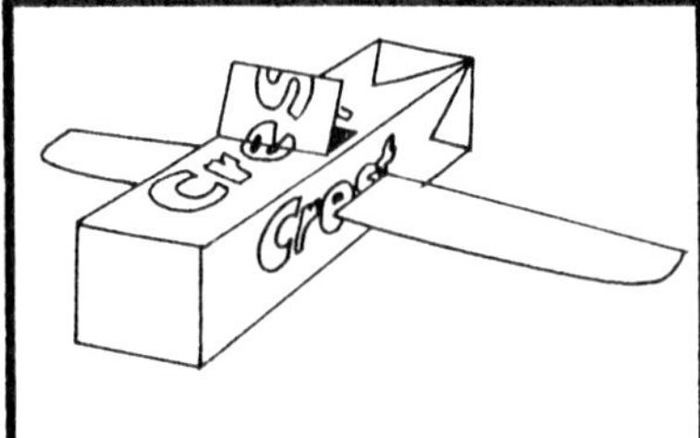

Insert a wing made out of cardboard through the two slots.

___

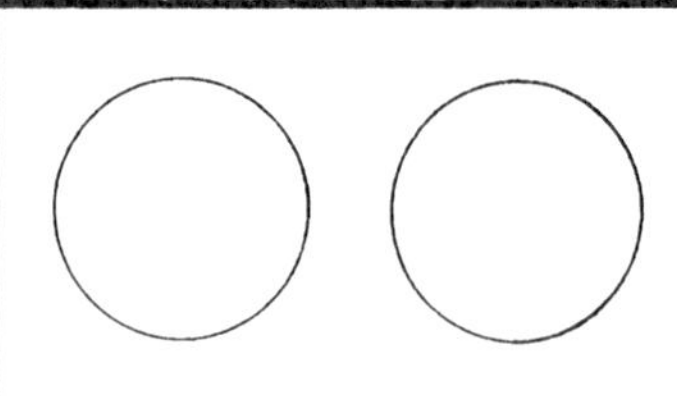

Finally, cut out cardboard circles about the size of a half dollar.

___

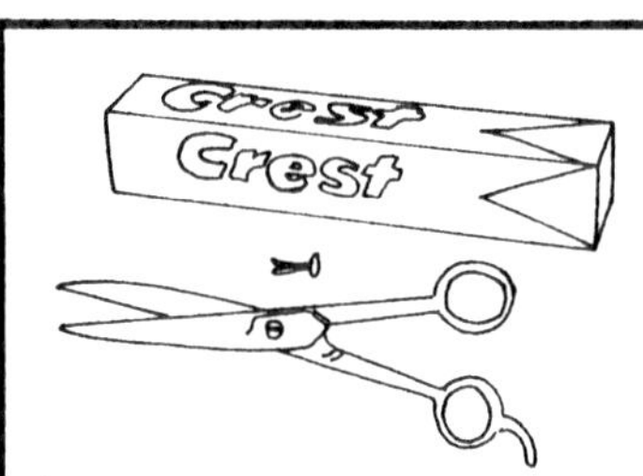

You will need a toothpaste box, scissors, a metal fastener, glue and cardboard.

___

Make a list of what you will need.

___

Second, make two slits opposite each other under the cockpit at the bottom of the box.

___

Glue the circles just in front of the wings.

___

Now follow the directions. If you numbered them correctly, you should be able to create a toothpaste box airplane.

- Circle the smallest measurement.

ounce   gram   kilogram   pound

Make a Balance Scale

Name ____________________

Number the sentences in order below to tell how to make a balance scale.

____ Punch a small hole where each inch line intersects the length line.

____ If the cardboard does not balance, cut off a little bit from the heavy end.

____ Trace around the ruler with a pencil.

____ After it is cut out, mark it off in eleven one-inch intervals beginning at zero and also draw a parallel line down its length, ¼ inch from the edge.

____ Make ten identical hooks out of small paper clips.

____ Put a twelve-inch ruler on a piece of cardboard.

____ Hang a paper clip from each of the ten holes.

____ Push a nail through the center line ½ inch above the intersecting line.

____ Cut the shape out of cardboard with heavy-duty scissors.

____ Rest the nail between two items of equal height such as glasses, empty cans, or books.

Number the pictures below to show the same order as above.

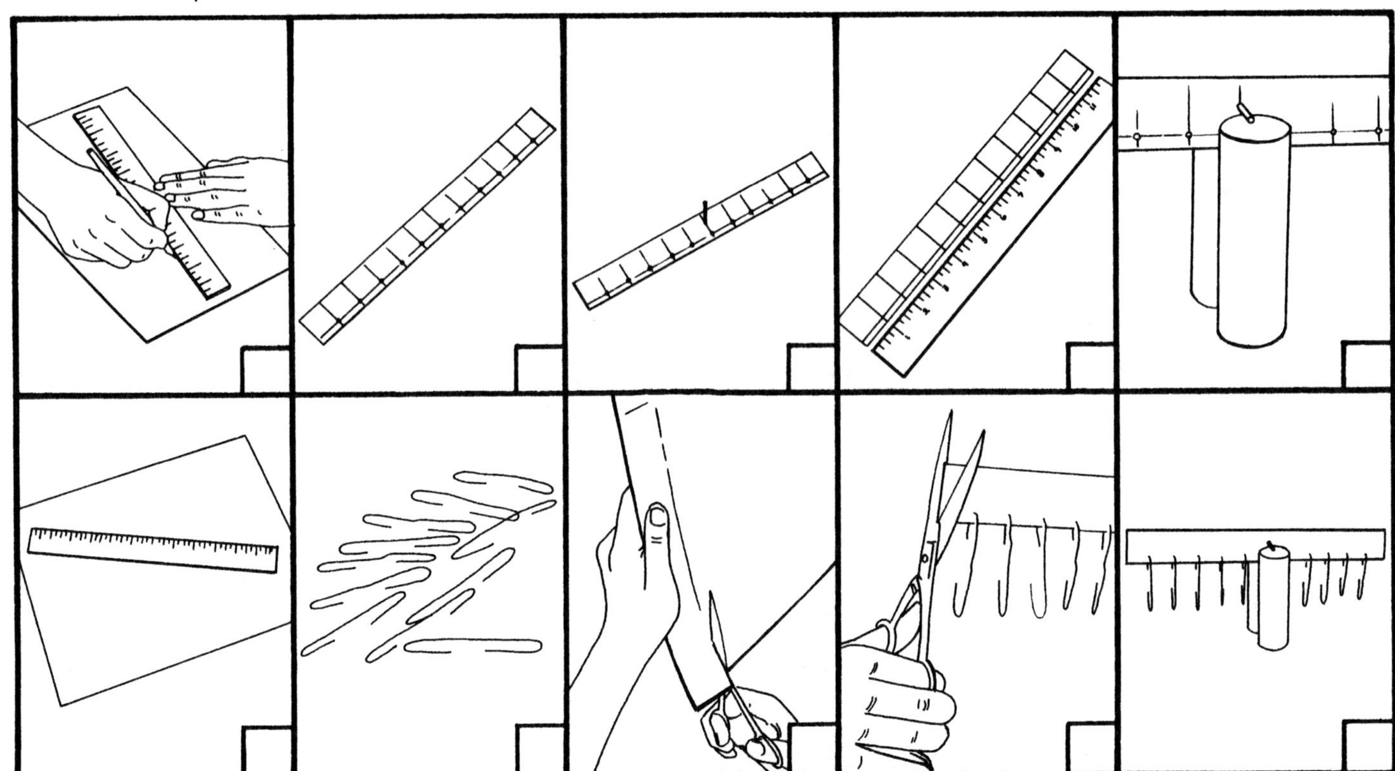

Try making a balance scale. If you do the above steps in order, it should work.

- Circle the largest measurement.

1 cup **4 tablespoons** **1 pint** **1 ounce**

What Next?

Name ______________________

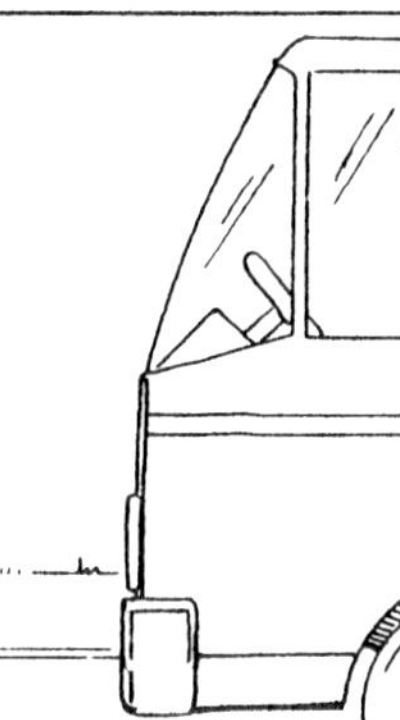

Complete each sentence by using an ending given in the box below.

1. The conductor raised his baton, and ______________
2. After all the money was counted, ______________
3. Doug decided that after high school graduation ______________
4. When the front gate is open, ______________
5. Betsy patted her dog and ______________
6. Melody waited at the bus stop until ______________
7. We worked on the decorations for ten hours today and ______________
8. Let's do our homework before dinner and ______________
9. The homesick boy cried quietly in bed until ______________
10. Every night when you're ready for bed ______________
11. Our guests took off their coats and ______________
12. I cleaned up the house before ______________

he'd go to college.	after dinner we will play outdoors.
we will work another ten tomorrow.	the dog sat at her side.
my dog runs away.	he fell asleep.
the orchestra played.	I will read a story to you.
it was deposited in the bank.	sat down.
the bus came.	I left for the office.

Make up your own beginnings for the following endings.

1. ______________ he tied up the boat.
2. ______________ and he began to snore.
3. ______________ and an argument followed.

- Circle the smallest amount of paper.

a quire **a ream** **a gross**

Skill: Support Sentences

Three Topics

Name ______________________________

The topic sentence for each paragraph is given. Find the support sentences for each paragraph and write them in order under the topic sentence to which they belong.

1. Jefferson won the athletic award at graduation for his accomplishments during his high school years. ______________________________

____

____

____

2. Our family is giving a surprise party for dad on his birthday. ______________________________

____

____

____

____

3. The teacher assigned each member of the class a different president on whom to make a report. ______________________________

____

____

____

Support Sentences

I'm going to ask Dad to stay and watch me play after he drives me to the baseball game.
In his senior year, he led the football team to the state championship.
During his first two years in high school, he was on every junior varsity team.
I don't know anything about him, so I'll have to go to the library to get some information.
While we're at the game, my mom and sister will decorate the house and bake a cake.
I'll write my report after I've collected my data.
In Jefferson's junior year, he broke four track records at the state meet.
When we get home our friends and family will be there.
I have to write a report on James Garfield.

- Circle the longest measurement.

circumference **diameter** **radius**

Related Activities

Name ______________________________

Describe at least two things you would do in each of the following circumstances.

Before going swimming	After going swimming
Before reading a book	After reading a book
Before going to the store	After going to the store
Before taking a test	After taking a test
Before shoveling snow	After shoveling snow
Before lighting a fire	After lighting a fire
Before signing an important document	After signing an important document
Before going on vacation	After going on vacation
Before grooming a pet	After grooming a pet

• Circle the least amount of money.

22 nickels 9 dimes 4 quarters 97 pennies

When It All Started

Name ____________________

Use the time line to decide if **before** or **after** should complete each statement.

1814 **Francis Scott Key wrote "The Star-Spangled Banner"**
1822 ***The Night Before Christmas* was written**
1845 **The Knickerbockers Club became the first organized baseball team**
1848 **First Woman's Rights Convention held**
1861 **The Civil War began**
1862 **Julia Ward Howe wrote "The Battle Hymn of the Republic"**
1873 **Football rules were formalized**
1881 **Clara Barton organized the American Red Cross**
1886 **The Statue of Liberty was given to America by France**
1892 **The Ferris wheel was invented**
1900 ***The Wizard of Oz* was published**
1902 **Teddy bears got their name from a cartoon of Teddy Roosevelt**
1912 **The Girl Scouts of America were founded**
1917 **The U.S. fought in World War I**
1921 **The first play-by-play baseball game was radio broadcasted**
1930 **Sliced bread and Twinkies were introduced**
1931 **The "Star-Spangled Banner" became the national anthem**
1950 **"Peanuts" comic strip was introduced**
1955 **Disneyland opens**
1960 **National Organization of Women (NOW) founded**

Baseball was organized __________ football.

"The Star-Spangled Banner" was written __________ The "Battle Hymn of the Republic."

The American Red Cross was organized __________ the Civil War.

"The Star-Spangled Banner" became the national anthem __________ World War I.

The Wizard of Oz was written __________ *The Night Before Christmas.*

The Girl Scouts of America began __________ the American Red Cross was founded.

Baseball was played __________ it was broadcast on the radio.

NOW was founded long __________ the first Woman's Rights Convention.

The name "teddy bear" originated __________ the Statue of Liberty was given to America.

The Ferris wheel was invented __________ Disneyland opened.

Sliced bread and Twinkies were introduced __________ World War I.

The first Woman's Rights Convention was held __________ the Civil War.

The Civil War took place __________ France gave America a gift.

- Circle the longest distance.

216 inches **20 feet** **7 yards**

Radio Waves

Name ______________________

Read the story. Then correctly complete each sentence below the story by writing **before** or **after** in the blanks.

Before 1900 there was no such thing as a radio. The telephone and telegraph had been invented. However, both of these inventions needed wires to send messages. Then a man in Germany found he could make radio waves with electric sparks that caused waves to move through the air without wires.

A small Italian boy named Guglielmo Marconi read about the German man's radio waves. He understood how they worked. He learned as much as he could about radio waves from books, though not much had been written about them at the time.

When Marconi was twenty years old, his father gave him two rooms on the top floor of the family home to use as a shop. Here, through trial and error, he found a way to send messages on the telegraph without wires. First he did it from one room to the next. Next he had his brother help him send a message down the street and then from one side of a hill to the other. Soon he was sending messages to locations over a mile away.

He needed money to continue his work. He asked the Italian government for it, but they refused his request. He decided to turn to another country and he took his work to England where he used the shop of a man also working on radio waves. Queen Victoria heard of Marconi's work and had him send messages to her from a boat on the water. At first the signals were weak, but the more he worked, the clearer they became. Finally he built a large antenna for sending and receiving signals across the Atlantic Ocean. The first radio message, three soft taps from England, was heard in Canada in 1901.

1. Radio waves were discovered __________ the telegraph was invented.
2. Marconi asked his government for money to further his work __________ he went to England.
3. Queen Victoria asked him to work for her __________ he moved to England.
4. Marconi worked for the Queen __________ sending a message across the ocean.
5. The radio was invented __________ the telephone.
6. Wires were needed to send messages __________ the radio was invented.
7. Marconi read all that he could about radio waves __________ he read about the German man's work.
8. Marconi had his brother help him __________ he sent messages from one room to another.

- Circle the three smallest numbers.

$12/4$ 15 $1/3$ $5/5$ .55 4^2

Getting the Bad Guys

Name ______________________________

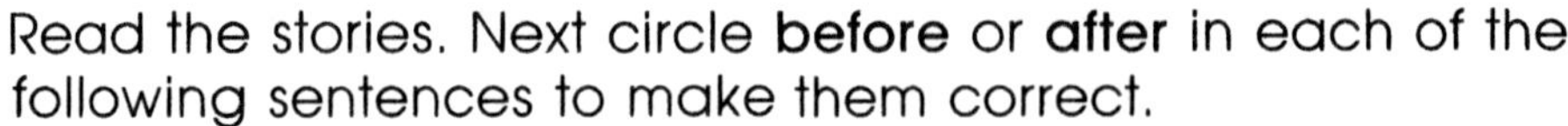

Read the stories. Next circle **before** or **after** in each of the following sentences to make them correct.

Not all men on the seas were pirates when piracy flourished. One such man was John Fillmore, a fisherman from Massachusetts, who was captured by a pirate ship when he was fishing. His choice was to join the outlaws or be killed. Rather than die, he joined them. After a few days he led a mutiny and seized the ship. He sailed the ship into Boston Harbor and turned it over to the authorities along with the captain and the crew. John Fillmore was a hero.

1. John Fillmore joined the pirates (before, after) he sailed into Boston Harbor.
2. John Fillmore was fishing (before, after) the pirate ship saw him.
3. The captain and his crew went to Boston (before, after) they captured John.
4. John seized the ship (before, after) he led a mutiny.
5. John was forced to be a pirate (before, after) he was a hero.
6. The captain and his crew gave John a choice (before, after) he was captured.

John Massey, an Englishman working as an engineer, was not as lucky as John Fillmore. On a voyage to Africa, he was forced to abandon his ship because the water supply ran out. He was stranded on an island until a pirate ship rescued him. He had little choice but to join the crew. When they landed in Jamaica, he jumped ship and helped the local authorities round up the crew. Jamaican authorities gave him letters praising his brave deeds, but when he returned to England they did not believe him. John Massey was executed for piracy.

1. John Massey rounded up the crew (before, after) he jumped ship.
2. John sailed to England (before, after) he had been a pirate.
3. The water supply on John's ship ran dry (before, after) he reached Africa.
4. The pirate ship saw John (before, after) he abandoned his ship.
5. John landed in Jamaica (before, after) he landed on an island.
6. England did not believe John even (before, after) they read the letters of praise from Jamaica.

- Circle the heaviest weight.

1 pound **12 ounces** **1 kilogram** **15 grams**

Set Them Straight

Name ______________________

Read each sentence. Write the part that happened first on the line following the word **FIRST**. Write the part that happened second on the line following the word **NEXT**.

Father hung the pictures that the children had painted.

FIRST ______________________

NEXT ______________________

Before the salesman removed the tags from the television set, he tested it to see that it worked.

FIRST ______________________

NEXT ______________________

John was chosen to give the speech at graduation because he had the highest grade point average.

FIRST ______________________

NEXT ______________________

By the time Karen reached the airport, the plane she was meeting had landed.

FIRST ______________________

NEXT ______________________

The dog was waiting on the front steps when I came home from school.

FIRST ______________________

NEXT ______________________

Jessie relaxed when she learned there would be no test.

FIRST ______________________

NEXT ______________________

The captain ordered the ship to travel ahead at full speed when the radio message warned that a storm was coming.

FIRST ______________________

NEXT ______________________

There had been heavy rains for a month so the farmers delayed their planting.

FIRST ______________________

NEXT ______________________

- Circle the measurement that is the third largest.

teaspoon cup tablespoon pint quart

The Missing Causes

Name ______________________

Find the missing cause for each sentence in the box at the bottom. Write it in the space.

1. ______________________ the baseball game will be played as scheduled.
2. Mother bought Jeanie a pretty pink dress because ______________________
____
3. I wasn't able to complete my math homework because ______________________
____
4. ______________________ and made it dark earlier than usual.
5. Carmen was upset when ______________________
6. Kathy was in pain because ______________________
7. ______________________ so we traded it in on a small economy car.
8. The suitcase was popping at the seams because ______________________
____
9. ______________________ caused its price to rise.
10. ______________________ helped Marcy get the leading role.
11. ______________________ and knocked down all the decorations.
12. The traffic light on the corner stopped working when ______________________

it was stuffed full of clothes.
If the ground is dry enough,
The cat climbed onto the mantel
The heavy cloud cover moved in quickly
he didn't get anything for Easter.
The great demand for copper tubing
Having long brown hair and brown eyes
she spilled paint on her other dress.
a car ran into it.
she stayed out in the sun too long.
Our truck only averaged twelve miles to the gallon
the last page of the assignment had been torn out of the textbook.

• Circle the city that is farthest from Washington, D.C.

Santa Fe **Chicago** **Philadelphia** **Miami**

Cause and Effect

Name ______________________________

Underline the **cause** in each sentence below.

1. The furnace was as old as the forty-year-old house and was in need of a lot of repair.
2. You never feel the rain in the rain forest because the trees are so thick they act like an umbrella.
3. The veteran racer was unable to complete the race when his car overturned on the far curve.
4. The kitchen sink backed up, and we couldn't do the dishes.
5. The heat rising in the hot air balloon made the balloon lift into the air and float over the treetops.
6. We went to the grocery store because our cupboard was bare.
7. After the electoral college votes were officially counted, the new President could take the oath of office.
8. Due to darkness, the tennis tournament had to be canceled.
9. The "T" key on the typewriter I used prints only the top half of the "T," so some of my words look strange.
10. I took a class in dog grooming so that Rover wouldn't look strange when I groomed him.

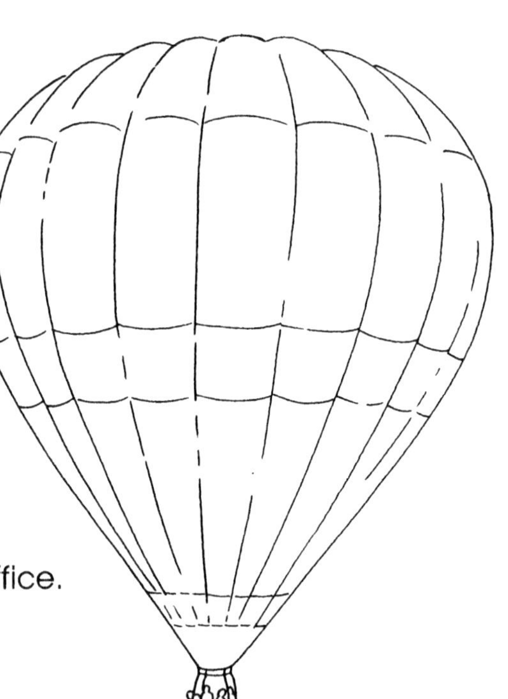

Underline the **effect** in each sentence below.

1. The siren that warns of bad storms sounded, and the students took their positions on the floor.
2. With two men on base, Harry hit a home run to give his team the lead.
3. Terry bought two pairs of boots because they were on sale, two for the price of one.
4. The tablecloth was sticky from the pickle relish and catsup.
5. The escaped prisoner was caught because he didn't follow the speed limit.
6. The red brick was beginning to show beneath the white coat of paint because the severe weather had washed most of it off.
7. I did very well on the test because I studied for it.
8. The late spring snow was heavy and it made the trees' branches bend to the ground.
9. When the fire went out, the house became cold.
10. Mother prepared father's favorite foods for dinner because it was his birthday.

• Circle the greatest number.

VII IX XX

So What Then?

Name ______________________________

Match the sentence parts that go together best. Write the number of the first part on the line in front of the last part for each one.

1. If you bake the cake,
2. If you close your eyes and count to ten,
3. If the Constitution of the United States had not been written,
4. If no one is on recess duty,
5. If you don't have a raincoat,
6. If you can't sit still now,
7. If the taxi doesn't come on time,
8. If Barbara has a green blouse,
9. If there are any leftovers,
10. If I am late for dinner,
11. If the students don't have permission slips,
12. If the schedule in the newspaper is correct,
13. If you tie a string on your finger,
14. If you see a penny, pick it up
15. If you don't answer the phone,
16. If the sun shines on the furniture,
17. If the children want ice cream,
18. If the music is too loud,
19. If the wind would stop blowing,
20. If there are more than forty people on the bus,

____ she should wear it on St. Patrick's Day.

____ I'll lend you one to wear during the storm.

____ they can't go on the field trip.

____ state governments might be responsible only to themselves.

____ and all the day you'll have good luck.

____ put down the awnings.

____ I'll make the icing.

____ you'll never be able to sit through the three-hour show.

____ it will help you remember.

____ you will be surprised at what you see when you open your eyes.

____ our neighbor will take us to the airport.

____ there will be many more accidents.

____ I will eat it cold.

____ they'll have to finish their meal.

____ move away from the speakers.

____ you will have to wait for the next one.

____ give them to the dog.

____ I'll know you went without me.

____ I'd go out for a walk.

____ the town meeting begins at 7:00 p.m.

• Which one shows 108? Circle it.

h	t	o
I	~~IIII~~ III	

h	t	o
I		~~IIII~~ II

h	t	o
I	~~IIII~~ III	~~IIII~~ III

h	t	o
I		~~IIII~~ III

Cause and Effect

Name ______________________________

Read the following sentences. Mark an X on the line in front of each sentence that has both a **cause** and an **effect**.

1. ____ The tree never grew tall because the rest of the forest kept sun and rain from reaching it.
2. ____ Five bands played in the parade before the football game.
3. ____ When the car reached 7,000 miles, it was due to have its first check.
4. ____ The ceiling in the living room dripped when father's tub ran over.
5. ____ After the movie, we went out for pizza and dessert.
6. ____ After the hot, dry summer, the river level was lower than it had ever been.
7. ____ On our way to Fred's farm, we saw a big accident.
8. ____ We roasted marshmallows and sang songs around the campfire before we got into our sleeping bags.
9. ____ The dog always barked at the sound of the doorbell.
10. ____ When the dentist cleaned my teeth, he said my mouth was in good shape.
11. ____ Chris was unhappy because he wasn't chosen to be on the soccer team.
12. ____ Maggie's piano recital was going to be next week so she began practicing every day after school until dinner was ready.
13. ____ If the house is too cool, turn up the heat.
14. ____ We went boating and swimming at the lake on our last day of vacation before we headed for home.
15. ____ Having a perfect paper makes me feel good.
16. ____ There has been an odor in the garage ever since the bag of fertilizer spilled on the floor.
17. ____ There are lots and lots of apples on the ground in the orchard.
18. ____ I wish we could have recess the rest of the day.
19. ____ The ambulance came in response to the 9-1-1 call.
20. ____ Trees were lying across the road after the tornado had come and gone.
21. ____ Traffic was so heavy we barely made it to school on time.
22. ____ Put your books, paper and pencil on your desk before we go to lunch.

- Circle the greatest amount.

.1 .5 .01 .05 .005 .001

In an Orderly Fashion

Name ______________________________

Number the sentences in order below to show how you would set a table.

____ Fold the napkins in half.
____ Set the dinner plates on the place mats.
____ Make sure your table is the right size to seat the number of people you expect for the meal.
____ Put the napkins to the left of the forks and set glasses directly above the knives and spoons.
____ Put the number of place mats you need around the table.
____ Put the forks to the left and the knives and spoons to the right of the dinner plates.

Number the sentences in order below to show how you would make a salad.

____ Place washed greens in a colander or on a towel to let the water drip off of them.
____ Sprinkle cheese on the top.
____ Place ingredients in a bowl and toss.
____ Pour dressing on when ready to serve and toss again.
____ Wash all fresh vegetables.
____ Cut all the vegetables into bite-size pieces.

Number the sentences in order below to show how you would make a bed.

____ Fold the top of the bedspread back to about eighteen inches from the head of the bed.
____ Tuck in the top sheet and blanket on three sides.
____ Lay the pillow at the head of the bed.
____ Put on the bottom fitted sheet.
____ Fold the top of the top sheet over the top of the blanket.
____ Fold the top of the bedspread back toward the head of the bed to cover the pillow.
____ Put on and spread the top sheet so its top touches the head of the bed and it hangs over the end and two sides.
____ Put on the bedspread so it hangs over the end and two sides.
____ Put on the blanket so it hangs over the foot of the bed and two sides.
____ Put on the mattress pad.

• Circle the largest amount.

millions **hundred thousands** **billions** **trillions**

Skill: Sequencing Events

Orderly Activities

Name ______________________________

Number the sentences in order below to tell how to change a tire.

____ Put the new tire on.
____ Put the tools and flat tire in the back of the car.
____ Pry off the hubcap with the tire iron.
____ Take out the necessary tools and spare tire.
____ Remove the flat tire.
____ Put the lug nuts back on and tighten them.
____ Remove the lug nuts with the other end of the tire iron.
____ Replace the hubcap.
____ Raise the car high enough so the weight is off the tire.

Number the sentences in order below to tell how to care for a cut.

____ Wash around the entire injured area with a little soap and warm water.
____ Select a bandage about the size of the wound.
____ A day later, check the wound and change the bandage.
____ Immediately put pressure on the wound to stop the bleeding.
____ Apply the bandage to the wound.
____ Clean the wound with disinfectant.
____ Put vaseline on the gauze part of the bandage to prevent it from sticking to the wound.

Number the sentences in order below to tell how to make lemonade.

____ Pour the lemon juice into an empty pitcher.
____ Determine how many glasses of lemonade you want to make.
____ Refrigerate until ready to use.
____ Cut the lemons in half.
____ Use one lemon for each glass of lemonade.
____ Pour lemonade in glasses and serve.
____ Squeeze the lemons.
____ Put ice in individual glasses.
____ Pour a cup of water and a tablespoon of sugar for each lemon used into the pitcher and stir the mixture.

• Circle the second smallest time span.

century **fortnight** **decade** **week**

Disasters

Name ______________________________

Number the sentences below in the order which best tells a story about the Chicago Fire.

____ As the night went on, more and more of the city burned as new fires were started by flying sparks and debris.

____ It had been very hot and dry in Chicago all through the summer and fall of 1871.

____ By the time the fire ended, there was nothing left to burn.

____ The hay inside the loft got so hot it exploded.

____ The dry weather and the fact that most of the city's buildings and sidewalks were made of wood made Chicago a kindling box.

____ The kerosene spilled, and flames quickly spread through the barn.

____ About a month later Chicago started to rebuild the city.

____ One Sunday evening in October of that year, Mrs. O'Leary went to her barn to look in on a sick cow.

____ Thousands were left homeless, and about 300 people lost their lives.

____ She set her kerosene lamp down, and one of her cows kicked it over.

____ Pieces of fiery wood and hay were blown by the winds, and soon other buildings in the area caught fire.

Number the sentences below in the order which best tells about Mount St. Helens.

____ Several more people began to leave the area, but a few curious individuals came to see what happened March 27, 1980.

____ In March of 1980, the mountain began to rumble.

____ Mount St. Helens is a very old volcano that first erupted over 2,000 years ago.

____ When it was over, rocks and ash covered an area of 150 square miles, and Mount St. Helens had lost 1,300 feet off its top.

____ Between 1857 and 1980 many small towns had developed near the mountain.

____ On May 18, 1980 there was another explosion, and hot gas and ash blew over eleven miles into the atmosphere.

____ Over the centuries it has erupted about once every 100 years.

____ On March 27, 1980 ash and steam were thrown four miles into the air.

____ Some of the residents in the area's small towns moved away.

____ The last time it erupted before 1980 was in 1857.

• Write the measurements in order from smallest to largest.

liter quart centiliter gallon ______________________________

The Early Years

Name ______________________________

Use the time line to help decide whether to write **true** or **false** before each statement below.

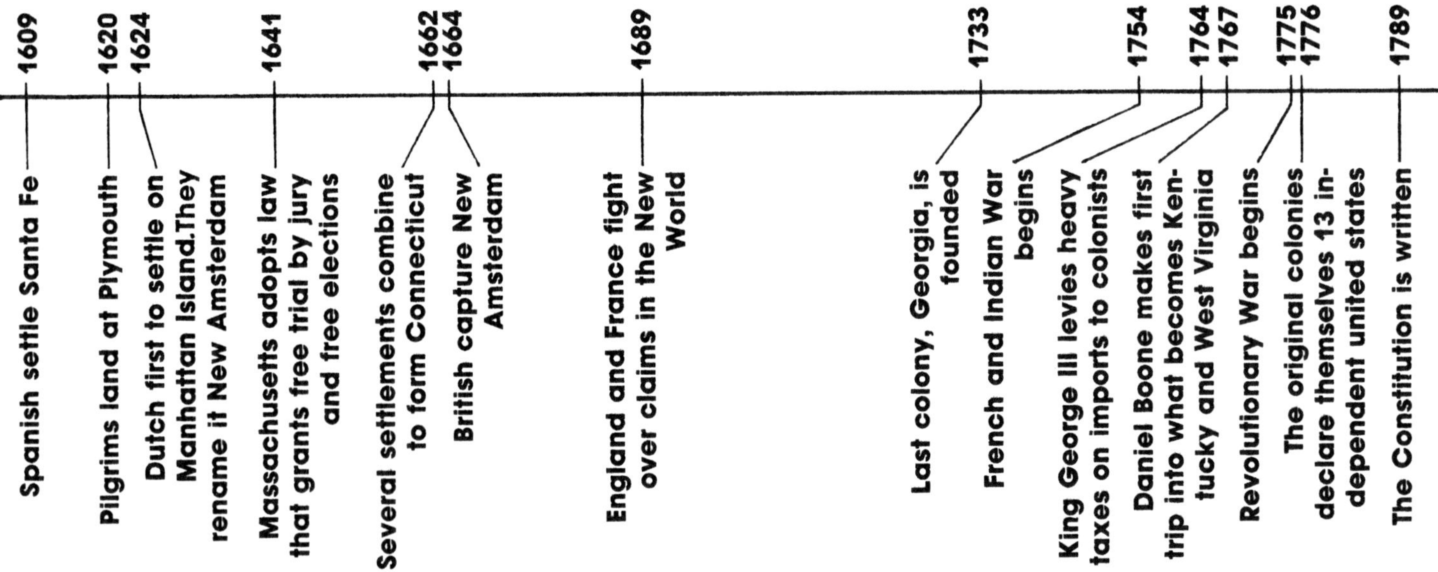

________ The British were the only European settlers in America.

________ America had no election laws until the Constitution was written.

________ The colonies became independent before the Revolutionary War began.

________ There were no wars on American soil until the Revolution.

________ The Dutch were the first Europeans to settle New Amsterdam.

________ All the original colonies were founded before the French and Indian Wars.

________ The first known Europeans to settle in Massachusetts were the Pilgrims.

________ No one ventured into the center part of the country until after the Revolution.

________ England and France fought over their claims in America before the last colony was established.

________ An Indian war was fought before the Revolution.

________ New Amsterdam belonged to the Dutch after 1664.

________ The colonists had to pay taxes to England before the Revolutionary War.

________ The French and Indian War took place before Daniel Boone explored the middle part of the country.

________ The Revolutionary War occurred after the Constitution was written.

• Circle the two smallest odd numbers.

16 60 24 12 9 36 45 25

Two American Authors

Name ________________________________

Read the following short biographies. Use the information in the biographies to fill in an abbreviated time line about each person. Write each year on the top line. Write the significant thing that happened that year on the lower line.

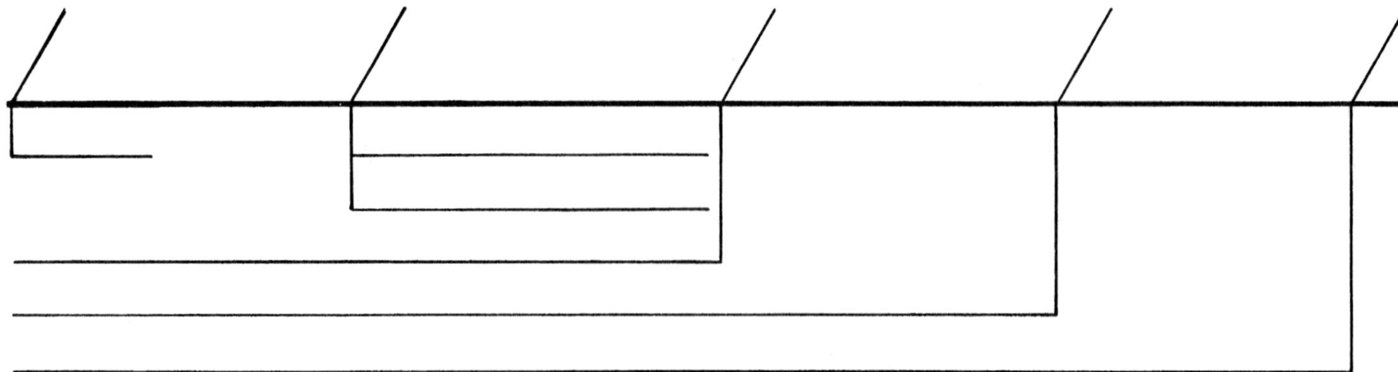

Mark Twain was born Samuel Langhorne Clemens in Florida, Missouri in 1835. He spent his early life moving from place to place with his family as his father went from job to job. His schooling ended when he was eleven and he was apprenticed to a printer. Through his work on newspapers, Samuel became inspired to write and study history. His work on riverboats on the Mississippi River around 1857 was a definite influence on his writings. His first book was published in 1867. In 1876 he gave *Tom Sawyer* to the world.

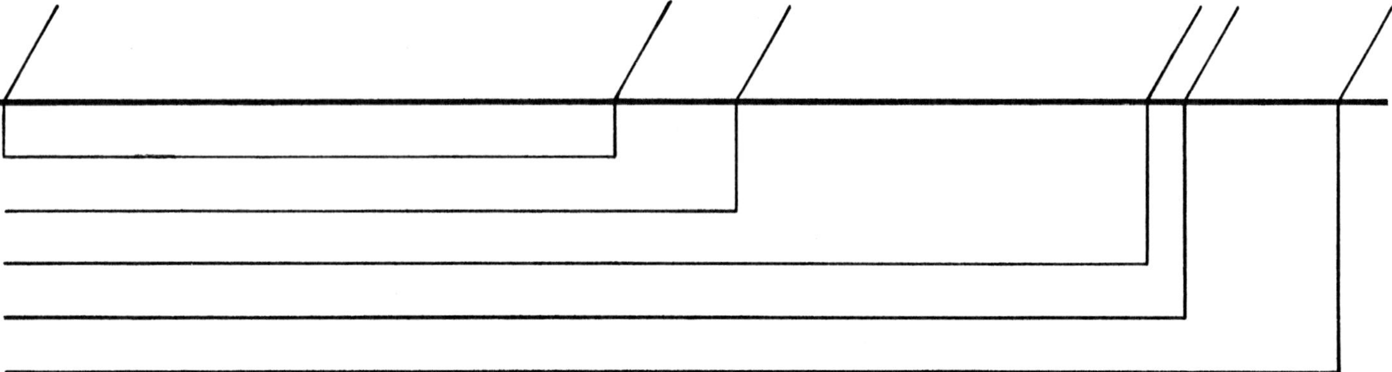

Harriet Beecher Stowe was born in 1811 into a family with an ever-present concern for improving humanity. Her father, a minister, had strong views about religion which she later questioned. In 1832 she moved with her family to Cincinnati where her father headed a new theological seminary, and in 1836 she married a professor from the school. She formulated strong antislavery views while at the school, and in 1850 she began to write about the slavery issue. In 1851 her *Uncle Tom's Cabin* began to appear as a serial in an abolitionist magazine. By the time the serial was completed, it had been published as a novel. She wrote a second antislavery novel in 1856, but she is best remembered for *Uncle Tom's Cabin*.

• Circle the longest period of time.

11:00 p.m.-midnight   11:00 p.m.-noon   noon-11:00 p.m.   midnight-11:00 a.m.

In Twenty-Seven Years

Name ______________________________

Read the following short history. Use the information to fill in the time line. Write each year on the top line. Write the significant thing that happened that year on the lower line.

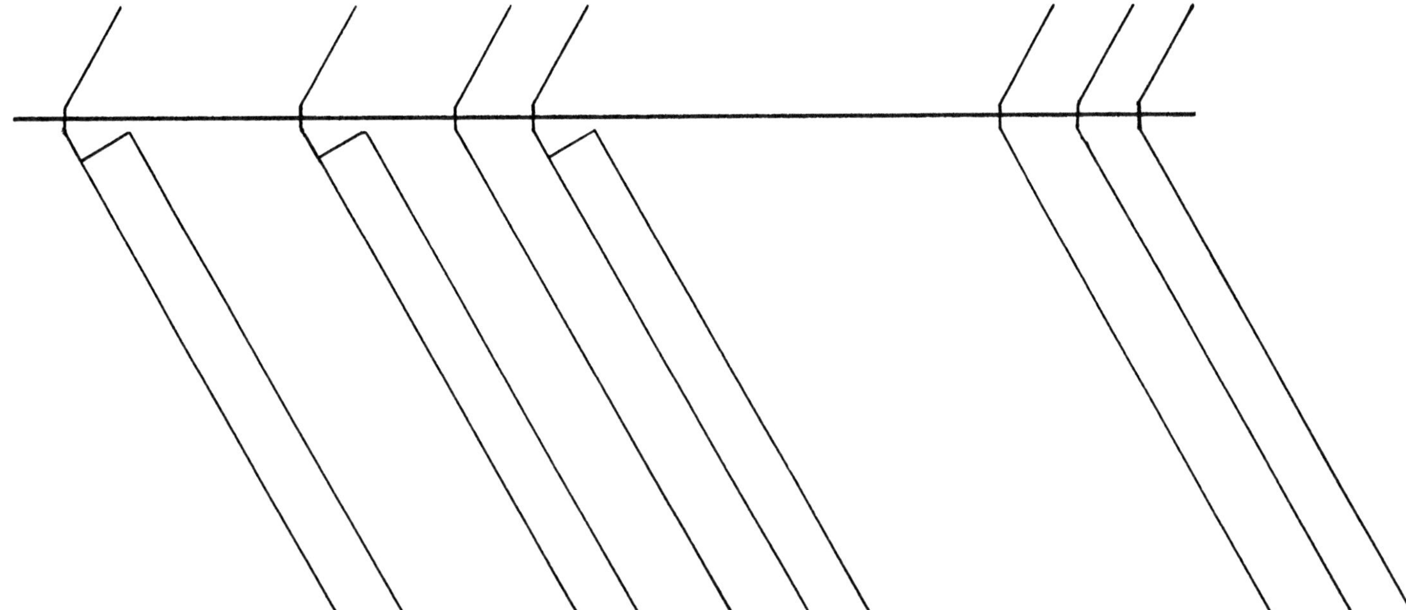

After America declared her independence, the Articles of Confederation were written in 1777. This document later became the first Constitution of the United States. It didn't work though because the states did not have to obey Congress. One problem occurred when the Revolutionary War ended in 1783. Many soldiers were penniless. The government had not paid them because it had no money. One article in the document specifically gave Congress the power to ask the states for money to pay soldier wages and other government expenses. But many of the states refused, and there was nothing Congress could do about it.

Four years after the war, fifty-five delegates met in Philadelphia for the purpose of changing the Articles. Instead, a whole new document, the Constitution, was written. The new Constitution set up two bodies of Congress. It stated that Congress would maintain an army and navy, deal with Indian affairs, operate a mail service, control trade, and establish and collect taxes. In the spring of 1789 the United States held its first elections under the new Constitution, and George Washington was elected President.

In 1801 Jefferson became President. When he took office, settlers in the West could no longer ship produce to New Orleans on the Mississippi because New Orleans belonged to France. Jefferson sent two men to Paris to negotiate with Napolean, a French general. Napoleon needed money to carry on his war with England, so, in 1803, he sold all the Louisiana territory to the United States for $15,000,000. The sale doubled the size of the United States. To find out what the territory included, Jefferson ordered Lewis and Clark to explore it and to find a water route across the Rockies. In the spring of 1804, they set out from St. Louis on a two-year, four-month expedition.

- Circle the shape that has the least number of sides.

octagon hexagon pentagon

Grooming a Horse

Name ______________________________

Read the story.

If you had a horse, the nicest thing you could do for it would be to groom it daily.

Grooming starts with the horse's feet. Each foot should be picked up and any dirt or stones should be removed with the point of the hoof pick. Work from the heel and move toward the toe. Before leaving the feet, check to see that the shoes fit and are on securely.

Use a dandy brush to loosen and remove caked dirt and sweat marks. Move the brush back and forth on the horse's body. Use a rubber curry comb on the back, belly and hip areas for the same purpose. The body brush has finer bristles which reach through to the skin. Use it on the head area and the body after most of the mud has been removed. Move the body brush in long, sweeping strokes, the same direction the horse's hair grows.

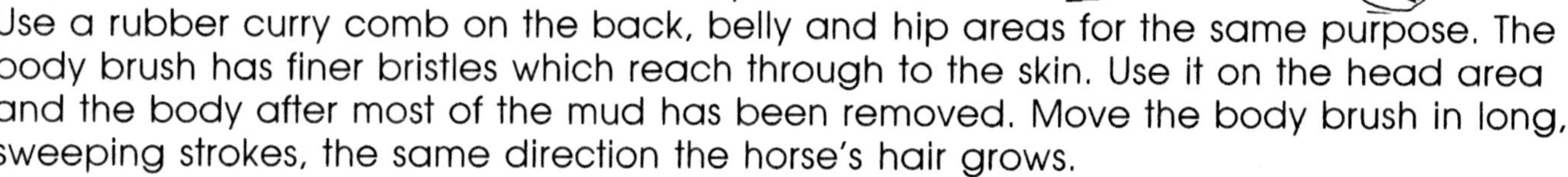

Once the horse is cleaned of dirt, use a soft, clean sponge to wipe the area around the eyes, nose and mouth. Dampen a rag and wipe any remaining dust from the horse's body.

The mane and tail should also be brushed, a few strands of hair at a time. Finally, put hoof oil on the outside of each hoof with a soft brush.

Number the sentences below to tell the best order to groom a horse.

____ Use a dandy brush and a rubber curry comb to clean the horse's body.

____ Wipe off any remaining dirt with a damp cloth.

____ Put oil on the horse's feet.

____ Clean under the horse's feet from heel to toe.

____ Brush the horse's mane and tail in sections.

____ Make sure the horse's shoes fit and are not loose.

____ After most of the dirt has been removed, use a body brush.

• Circle the greatest amount.

a liter **a gallon** **a pint** **a quart**

Beginning Karate

Name ______________________________

Read the information.

Fighting stances are basic to the art of karate. Stances are special standing positions from which various fighting techniques are performed.

The horse stance is the simplest one. It can be used for either attack or defense. It allows for a great deal of flexibility because you can move easily from it to any of the other stances.

To do the horse stance, you first must spread your feet apart and bend your knees, much as you would if you were riding a horse. Point your toes inward toward the opening between your legs. Both hands should be made into fists, then held at the waist, palms up. The upper half of your body should be straight up and down. Your weight should be evenly distributed between both legs. From this stance you are ready to move into other stances and movements.

Number the sentences in order below to tell about the beginning stages of karate.

____ Keep the upper part of your body erect.

____ Keep your hands at your waist.

____ You have to learn the stances of karate before you can advance to the next stages.

____ To learn the horse stance, first stand with your feet apart.

____ To keep your balance, your weight should be evenly distributed on both feet.

____ The least complicated stance is the horse stance.

____ Bend your knees and sit back as though you were sitting on a horse.

____ Make fists with your hands.

____ Your toes should be turned in.

____ The palm side of each hand should be up.

- Circle the smallest fraction.

2/5 3/6 1/2 1/3 3/7

Rodeo

Name ______________________________

Fill in the missing information for the following paragraphs. Use the sentences given in the box at the bottom.

The word rodeo comes from a Spanish word meaning round-up. Today's rodeo events come from the skills cowboys once needed during round-ups. Every ranch had untamed horses called broncos. ____

There were no arenas or time limits like there are today. ____ This was exciting and it drew a lot of spectators, so someone decided to charge admission. That is how the rodeo got started.

Today there are rodeos throughout the United States with many events in addition to bronco-riding. ____ Rodeo events are not just for cowboys. Women and children participate too.

Many of the rodeo performers are professionals. ____

The contestants do not take home much money after they've paid traveling expenses and entry fees. ____

> Cowboys would challenge one another to bronco-riding contests for amusement.
> If they win enough money to break even, they are doing well.
> They spend a lot of time on the road traveling from one rodeo to another.
> A cowboy would get on a wild horse and ride it until it stopped bucking or until he landed in the dirt.
> Roping, bull–riding, steer wrestling and barrel racing are also performed.

- Circle the greatest volume.

dry quart **bushel** **dry pint** **peck**

Fossils

Name ______________________________

Fill in the missing information for the following paragraphs. Use the sentences given in the box at the bottom.

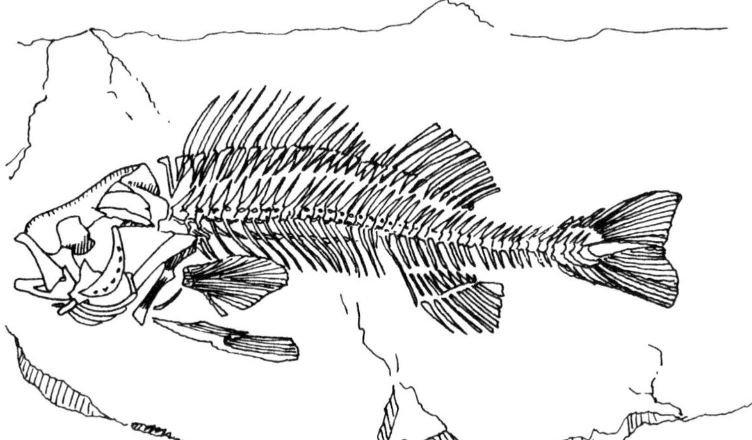

Hundreds of thousands of years ago there were millions of plants and animals living on earth, many of them different from those we know today. ______________________________
____
____
____

Some fossils are actually imprints of ancient plants and animals that left their marks in clay. The clay later hardened into rock. ______________________________
____

An animal or plant may become a fossil only if some part of it is hard enough to be preserved. ______________________________
____
______________________________ Other conditions must also be right. The hard part of the plant or animal must be buried quickly and left undisturbed. Otherwise it will decay. Many of the plants and animals that are now fossils were preserved when their hard parts changed into different substances. ______________________________
______________________________ When the water evaporated, the minerals remained and made the bones, shells and wood harder.

Most animals and plants vanished without leaving a trace of themselves, but those that didn't, left treasures for people to find — now and in the future.

> Other fossils are the remains of a plant or animal that have turned to stone.
> Water that had minerals in it was soaked up by the bone, shell or wood.
> The hard parts like bone, shell or wood decay more slowly, and therefore form a mold for replacement minerals.
> We know they lived on earth because they left records that we call fossils.

- Circle which is the greatest.

3 hundreds **40 tens** **12 tens and 9 ones**

Land Recycling

Name ______________________________

Fill in the missing information for the following paragraphs. Use the sentences given in the box at the bottom.

New land is sometimes built by volcanic action. Lava from deep within the earth may flow up slowly or spurt out with great force to form new land. ______________________________
____
____
Some mountain ranges have been formed in this way.

As the land forms it also vanishes. There are different kinds of weathering forces that make the land disappear. ____
______________________________ It is usually very slow and not too easy to see.
____
____
Another force is easier to see. ____
One example of physical weathering is when rainwater carves canyons as it carries away the land. Another example is when wind beating against rocks breaks boulders into smaller and smaller pieces until they become sand. ______________________________
____ Rocks may expand when heated by the sun during the day and shrink when cooled at night. When they cool, they may crack and rainwater may move into the crack. This will start physical weathering. While the weathering is occurring, so is the building of the land in a continuous cycle.

It is called physical weathering. One is called chemical weathering. New land also forms when the hot matter inside the earth pulls the crust of the earth and causes it to wrinkle and crack. It happens when two gases in the air (oxygen and carbon dioxide) attack the chemicals in the earth's rocks and soil. A third way land disappears is when it is heated and cooled.

- Circle the year that is furthest back in time.

3500 B.C. **A.D. 1620** **500 B.C.** **A.D. 200**

Star Light, Star Bright

Name ______________________________

Read the following paragraph about stars. Its sentences are out of order so rewrite it on the lines below in the correct order. Begin by telling about the smallest stars.

The second largest stars in size are called giant stars. Most stars are about the same size as the sun, which is considered to be a medium-sized star. White dwarfs, the second smallest stars in size, are smaller than the distance across Asia. The smallest stars are called neutron stars. The largest size stars are called supergiants; they are more than 1,000 times the size of the sun.

Draw pictures of each of the different-sized stars from largest to smallest and label each one.

- Circle the lightest measurement.

an ounce **a gram** **a pound** **a dram**

Sequences

Name ______________________________

Write in the missing letters for each sequence. On the line below it, write the category for each sequence.

1. T ___ ___ ___ TY, ___ ___ ___ ETE ___ ___ , E ___ ___ ___ ___ ___ EN, ___ ___ ___ ___ ___ TEEN

   ____

2. M ___ ___ DA ___ , ___ UE ___ ___ ___ Y, W ___ ___ ___ ___ S ___ ___ ___ ,
   T ___ ___ ___ ___ ___ ___ ___

   ____

3. ___ UG ___ ___ ___ , ___ ___ PT ___ ___ ___ ER, ___ C ___ ___ ___ E ___ ,
   N ___ ___ ___ ___ B ___ R

   ____

4. Y ___ ___ R, ___ ONT ___ , ___ ___ ___ K, ___ A ___ , H ___ ___ ___ , ___ I ___ ___ TE

   ____

5. A ___ ___ L ___ , ___ A ___ A ___ A, C ___ NT ___ L ___ UP ___ , D ___ ___ E

   ____

6. ___ ___ ___ TH, Y ___ ___ ___ , D ___ C ___ ___ E, C ___ ___ ___ UR ___

   ____

• Circle the most recent year.

A.D. 1776 **3000 B.C.** **A.D. 1801** **1200 B.C.**

Sequence Words

Name ______________________________

Circle the sequence word or words in each sentence.

1. The first thing I did when I got home was take off my shoes.
2. The guests arrived at Dan's surprise party fifteen minutes ahead of time.
3. It will soon be time for Aunt Meg and Uncle Jack to leave for the airport.
4. The boy in front of Bill cut in line.
5. Every fifth person in the lunch line got an extra cookie.
6. Father had to wait for me to pick him up because his train got in early.
7. We can watch television after dinner.
8. Father waited until dark before he went fishing.
9. The premature baby weighed 2½ pounds.
10. The boy scouts carried the flag at the head of the parade.
11. Formerly we received notices to let us know the meetings were to be held.
12. A letter was sent out by City Hall prior to closing off Main Street.
13. The room had previously been painted pink.
14. The teacher was behind her desk.
15. It started to rain Tuesday, and it continued for five succeeding days.
16. The weatherman said snow is expected tomorrow.
17. No one has been in the attic since the fire.
18. Turn to the following page to find the answer to the riddle.
19. The letter must be mailed immediately.
20. A vote was taken in closed session preceding the general convention.
21. We went on a picnic yesterday.
22. Sally was the second one to complete her work.
23. The President's speech was sent to the press in advance of its telecast.
24. The doctor saw me sooner than he expected.
25. The award was given posthumously to the soldier's family.
26. Bring me the needle and thread now and I will sew the button on your shirt.
27. The scout troop was in the rear car of the train.
28. The next batter hit a homerun and tied the game.
29. Casey came in last in the contest.
30. I will call you later to let you know when the movie starts.

- Circle the longest measurement.

a decimeter **a meter** **a foot** **a yard**

Sequence Crossword

Name ____________________

Complete the puzzle by writing the missing sequence word from each sentence below. The first one has been done for you.

				[1]B					[2]		
	[3]L	A	T	E	R		[4]	H			
			[5]								
										[6]P	
							[7]	[8]			
			[9]								
	[10]										
					[11]						
[12]		[13]						Y			
					[14]						
[15]		C									

Across

3. Jim arrived ________ than anyone else.
4. We set our clocks ________ one hour when daylight savings time began.
5. The person who comes into the room ________ should open the windows.
7. You go to the ________ of the line.
10. Andy was at the ________ of the class.
12. There were no clues about the missing puppy as of ________ afternoon.
14. Give me your money ________ and I'll buy the tickets.
15. Harrison sits in the ________ of the room so he won't get called on.

Down

1. The eggs were hidden ________ the barn.
2. He put his books ________ to the teacher's desk.
4. There is no sense in locking the gate ________ the horse has gotten out.
6. Jamie bought his airplane ticket ________ to the departure date.
8. One of Benjamin Franklin's proverbs begins, " ________ to bed . . ."
9. Ed's name was ________ on the list.
11. The boys stood in ________ when they posed for the family picture.
13. Jeff has gone hunting three times ________ duck hunting season began.

- Circle the year that is furthest back in time.

800 B.C. **400 B.C.** **A.D. 59** **1200 B.C.**

The Language of Sequencing

Name ______________________

Write a sentence using each of the sequence words or phrases given below.

1. in back of ______________________
2. beforehand ______________________
3. after ______________________
4. in front of ______________________
5. preceding ______________________
6. prior to ______________________
7. sooner ______________________
8. lower than ______________________
9. in advance of ______________________
10. second from the ______________________
11. since ______________________
12. succeeding ______________________

Choose two sequence words that have not been used above. Use each one in a separate sentence. Circle your sequence words.

1. ______________________
2. ______________________

- Circle the largest music group.

trio **sextet** **septet** **duet** **quartet**

Answer Key
Sequencing
Grade 5

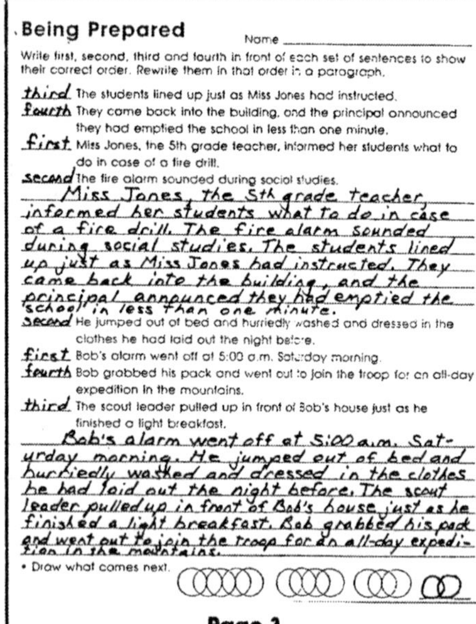

Being Prepared Name ______

Write first, second, third and fourth in front of each set of sentences to show their correct order. Rewrite them in that order in a paragraph.

third The students lined up just as Miss Jones had instructed.
fourth They came back into the building, and the principal announced they had emptied the school in less than one minute.
first Miss Jones, the 5th grade teacher, informed her students what to do in case of a fire drill.
second The fire alarm sounded during social studies.

Miss Jones, the 5th grade teacher, informed her students what to do in case of a fire drill. The fire alarm sounded during social studies. The students lined up just as Miss Jones had instructed. They came back into the building, and the principal announced they had emptied the school in less than one minute.

second He jumped out of bed and hurriedly washed and dressed in the clothes he had laid out the night before.
first Bob's alarm went off at 5:00 a.m. Saturday morning.
fourth Bob grabbed his pack and went out to join the troop for an all-day expedition in the mountains.
third The scout leader pulled up in front of Bob's house just as he finished a light breakfast.

Bob's alarm went off at 5:00 a.m. Saturday morning. He jumped out of bed and hurriedly washed and dressed in the clothes he had laid out the night before. The scout leader pulled up in front of Bob's house just as he finished a light breakfast. Bob grabbed his pack and went out to join the troop for an all-day expedition in the mountains.

• Draw what comes next.

Page 3

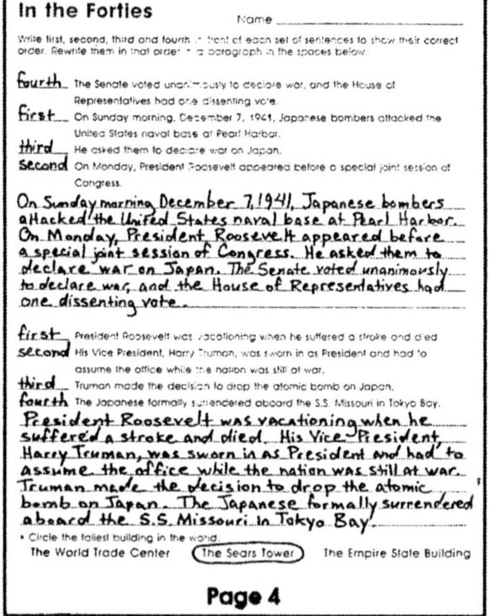

In the Forties Name ______

Write first, second, third and fourth in front of each set of sentences to show their correct order. Rewrite them in that order in a paragraph in the spaces below.

fourth The Senate voted unanimously to declare war, and the House of Representatives had one dissenting vote.
first On Sunday morning, December 7, 1941, Japanese bombers attacked the United States naval base at Pearl Harbor.
third He asked them to declare war on Japan.
second On Monday, President Roosevelt appeared before a special joint session of Congress.

On Sunday morning December 7, 1941, Japanese bombers attacked the United States naval base at Pearl Harbor. On Monday, President Roosevelt appeared before a special joint session of Congress. He asked them to declare war on Japan. The Senate voted unanimously to declare war, and the House of Representatives had one dissenting vote.

first President Roosevelt was vacationing when he suffered a stroke and died.
second His Vice President, Harry Truman, was sworn in as President and had to assume the office while the nation was still at war.
third Truman made the decision to drop the atomic bomb on Japan.
fourth The Japanese formally surrendered aboard the S.S. Missouri in Tokyo Bay.

President Roosevelt was vacationing when he suffered a stroke and died. His Vice President, Harry Truman, was sworn in as President and had to assume the office while the nation was still at war. Truman made the decision to drop the atomic bomb on Japan. The Japanese formally surrendered aboard the S.S. Missouri in Tokyo Bay.

• Circle the tallest building in the world.
The World Trade Center (The Sears Tower) The Empire State Building

Page 4

Stories in Nature Name ______

Number the pictures in order to make a story.

2 1 3 4

Write sentences that tell about the pictures in the order you numbered them.

Answers will vary.

Number these pictures also to make a story.

2 4 1 3

Write sentences that tell about the pictures in the order you numbered them.

Answers will vary.

• Circle the latest time.
half past 3 o'clock p.m. (3:41 p.m.) 20 minutes to 4:00 p.m.

Page 5

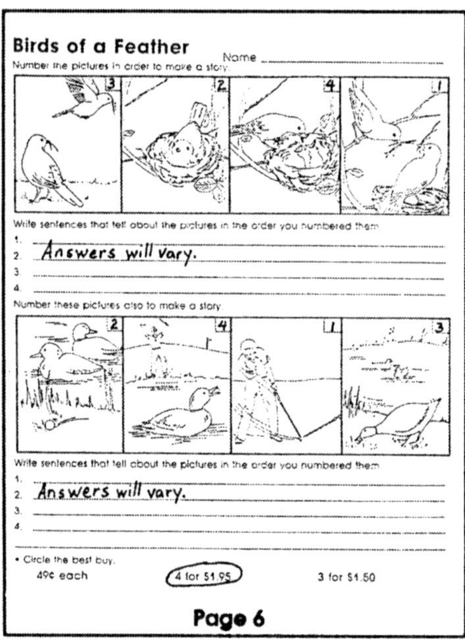

Birds of a Feather Name ______

Number the pictures in order to make a story.

3 2 4 1

Write sentences that tell about the pictures in the order you numbered them.

1.
2. Answers will vary.
3.
4.

Number these pictures also to make a story.

2 4 1 3

Write sentences that tell about the pictures in the order you numbered them.

1.
2. Answers will vary.
3.
4.

• Circle the best buy.
49¢ each (4 for $1.95) 3 for $1.50

Page 6

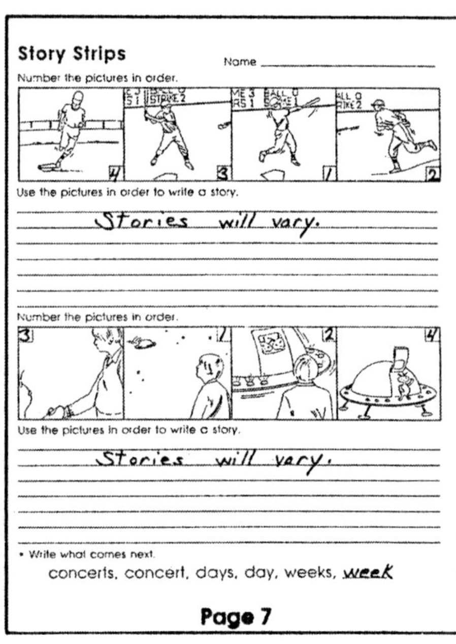

Story Strips Name ______

Number the pictures in order.

4 3 1 2

Use the pictures in order to write a story.

Stories will vary.

Number the pictures in order.

3 1 2 4

Use the pictures in order to write a story.

Stories will vary.

• Write what comes next.
concerts, concert, days, day, weeks, week

Page 7

A Long Tale

Name ______________

Number the pictures in order to make a story.

3 7 4 2
1 5 8 6

Write a story following the order you numbered the pictures.

Story will vary.

• Draw what comes next.

Page 8

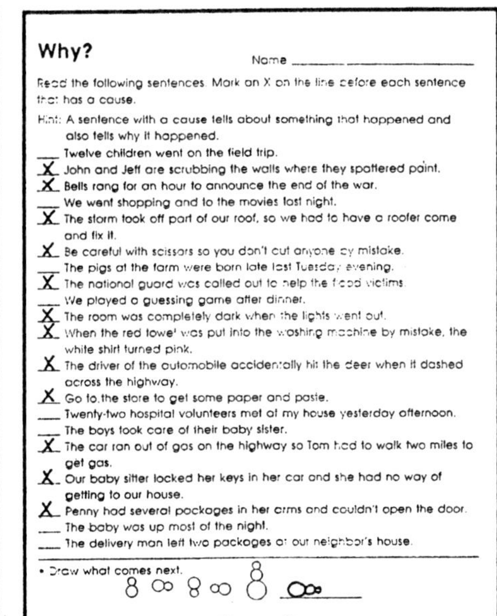

Why?

Name ______________

Read the following sentences. Mark an X on the line before each sentence that has a cause.

Hint: A sentence with a cause tells about something that happened and also tells why it happened.

___ Twelve children went on the field trip.
X John and Jeff are scrubbing the walls where they spattered paint.
X Bells rang for an hour to announce the end of the war.
___ We went shopping and to the movies last night.
X The storm took off part of our roof, so we had to have a roofer come and fix it.
X Be careful with scissors so you don't cut anyone by mistake.
___ The pigs at the farm were born late last Tuesday evening.
X The national guard was called out to help the flood victims.
___ We played a guessing game after dinner.
X The room was completely dark when the lights went out.
X When the red towel was put into the washing machine by mistake, the white shirt turned pink.
X The driver of the automobile accidentally hit the deer when it dashed across the highway.
X Go to the store to get some paper and paste.
___ Twenty-two hospital volunteers met at my house yesterday afternoon.
___ The boys took care of their baby sister.
X The car ran out of gas on the highway so Tom had to walk two miles to get gas.
X Our baby sitter locked her keys in her car and she had no way of getting to our house.
X Penny had several packages in her arms and couldn't open the door.
___ The baby was up most of the night.
___ The delivery man left two packages at our neighbor's house.

• Draw what comes next.

Page 9

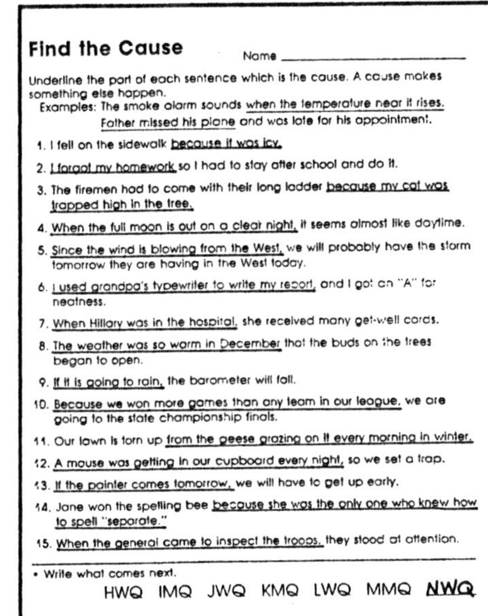

Find the Cause

Name ______________

Underline the part of each sentence which is the cause. A cause makes something else happen.

Examples: The smoke alarm sounds when the temperature near it rises.
Father missed his plane and was late for his appointment.

1. I fell on the sidewalk because it was icy.
2. I forgot my homework so I had to stay after school and do it.
3. The firemen had to come with their long ladder because my cat was trapped high in the tree.
4. When the full moon is out on a clear night, it seems almost like daytime.
5. Since the wind is blowing from the West, we will probably have the storm tomorrow they are having in the West today.
6. I used grandpa's typewriter to write my report, and I got an "A" for neatness.
7. When Hillary was in the hospital, she received many get-well cards.
8. The weather was so warm in December that the buds on the trees began to open.
9. If it is going to rain, the barometer will fall.
10. Because we won more games than any team in our league, we are going to the state championship finals.
11. Our lawn is torn up from the geese grazing on it every morning in winter.
12. A mouse was getting in our cupboard every night, so we set a trap.
13. If the painter comes tomorrow, we will have to get up early.
14. Jane won the spelling bee because she was the only one who knew how to spell "separate."
15. When the general came to inspect the troops, they stood at attention.

• Write what comes next.

HWQ IMQ JWQ KMQ LWQ MMQ NWQ

Page 10

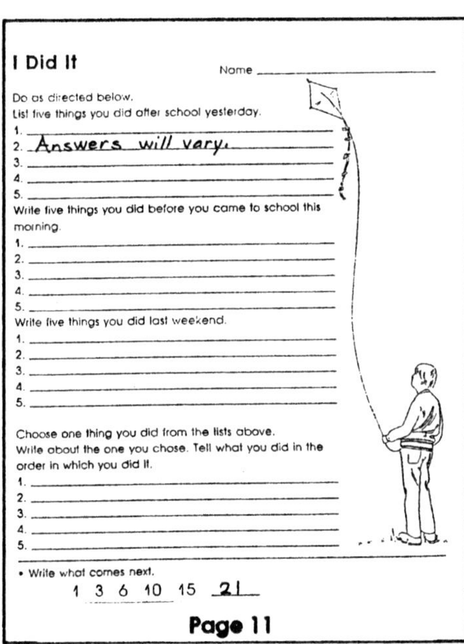

I Did It

Name ______________

Do as directed below.

List five things you did after school yesterday.

1.
2. Answers will vary.
3.
4.
5.

Write five things you did before you came to school this morning.

1.
2.
3.
4.
5.

Write five things you did last weekend.

1.
2.
3.
4.
5.

Choose one thing you did from the lists above. Write about the one you chose. Tell what you did in the order in which you did it.

1.
2.
3.
4.
5.

• Write what comes next.

1 3 6 10 15 21

Page 11

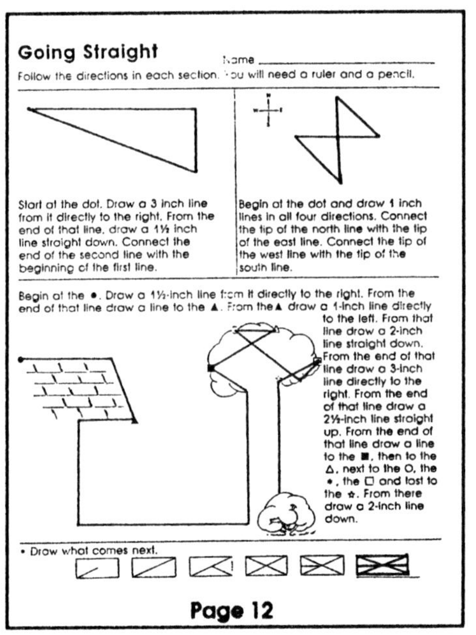

Going Straight

Name ______________

Follow the directions in each section. You will need a ruler and a pencil.

Start at the dot. Draw a 3 inch line from it directly to the right. From the end of that line, draw a 1½ inch line straight down. Connect the end of the second line with the beginning of the first line.

Begin at the dot and draw 1 inch lines in all four directions. Connect the tip of the north line with the tip of the east line. Connect the tip of the west line with the tip of the south line.

Begin at the •. Draw a 1½-inch line from it directly to the right. From the end of that line draw a line to the ▲. From the ▲ draw a 1-inch line directly to the left. From that line draw a 2-inch line straight down. From the end of that line draw a 3-inch line directly to the right. From the end of that line draw a 2½-inch line straight up. From the end of that line draw a line to the ■, then to the △, next to the O, the •, the □ and last to the ☆. From there draw a 2-inch line down.

• Draw what comes next.

Page 12

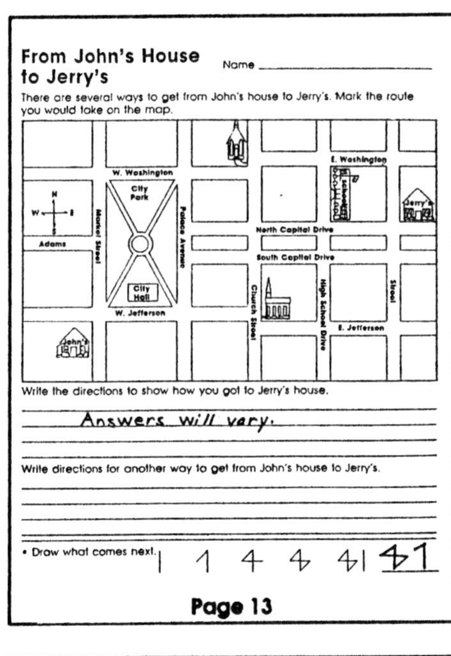

From John's House to Jerry's

Name ______________

There are several ways to get from John's house to Jerry's. Mark the route you would take on the map.

Write the directions to show how you got to Jerry's house.

Answers will vary.

Write directions for another way to get from John's house to Jerry's.

• Draw what comes next.

Page 13

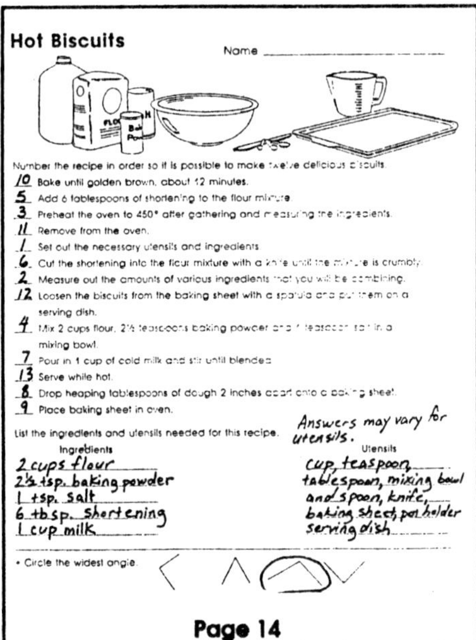

Hot Biscuits

Name ______________

Number the recipe in order so it is possible to make twelve delicious biscuits.

10 Bake until golden brown, about 12 minutes.
5 Add 6 tablespoons of shortening to the flour mixture.
3 Preheat the oven to 450° after gathering and measuring the ingredients.
11 Remove from the oven.
1 Set out the necessary utensils and ingredients.
6 Cut the shortening into the flour mixture with a knife until the mixture is crumbly.
2 Measure out the amounts of various ingredients that you will be combining.
12 Loosen the biscuits from the baking sheet with a spatula and put them on a serving dish.
4 Mix 2 cups flour, 2½ teaspoons baking powder and 1 teaspoon salt in a mixing bowl.
7 Pour in 1 cup of cold milk and stir until blended.
13 Serve while hot.
8 Drop heaping tablespoons of dough 2 inches apart onto a baking sheet.
9 Place baking sheet in oven.

List the ingredients and utensils needed for this recipe. Answers may vary for utensils.

Ingredients	Utensils
2 cups flour	cup, teaspoon
2½ tsp. baking powder	tablespoon, mixing bowl
1 tsp. salt	and spoon, knife,
6 tbsp. shortening	baking sheet, pot holder
1 cup milk	serving dish

• Circle the widest angle.

Page 14

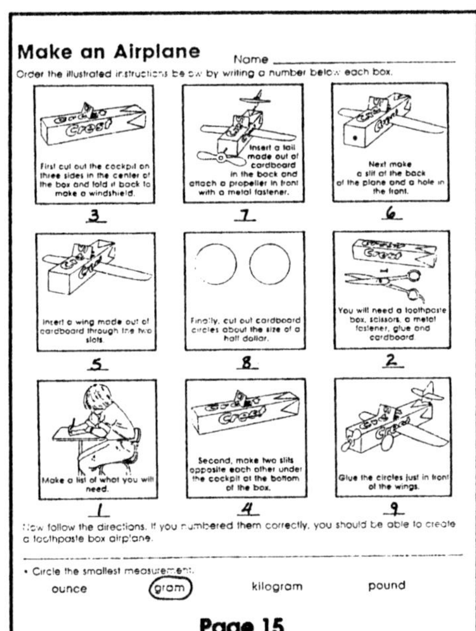

Make an Airplane

Name ______________

Order the illustrated instructions below by writing a number below each box.

First cut out the cockpit on three sides in the center of the box and fold it back to make a windshield. — 3

Insert a tail made out of cardboard in the back and attach a propeller in front with a metal fastener. — 7

Next make a slit at the back of the plane and a hole in the front. — 6

Insert a wing made out of cardboard through the two slots. — 5

Finally, cut out cardboard circles about the size of a half dollar. — 8

You will need a toothpaste box, scissors, a metal fastener, glue and cardboard. — 2

Make a list of what you will need. — 1

Second, make two slits opposite each other under the cockpit at the bottom of the box. — 4

Glue the circles just in front of the wings. — 9

Now follow the directions. If you numbered them correctly, you should be able to create a toothpaste box airplane.

• Circle the smallest measurement.

ounce (gram) kilogram pound

Page 15

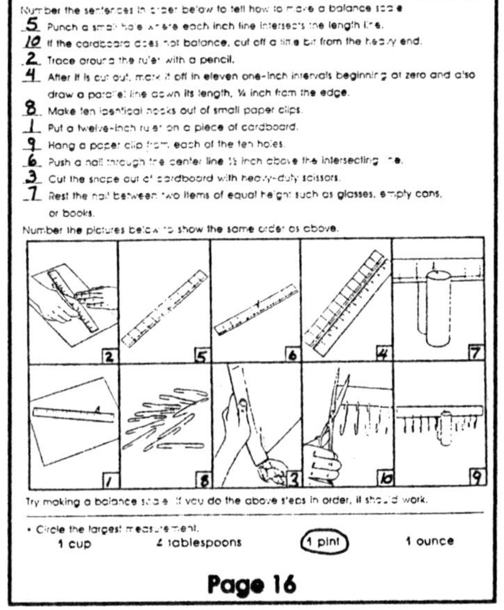

Make a Balance Scale

Name ______________

Number the sentences in order below to tell how to make a balance scale.

5 Punch a small hole where each inch line intersects the length line.
10 If the cardboard does not balance, cut off a little bit from the heavy end.
2 Trace around the ruler with a pencil.
4 After it is cut out, mark it off in eleven one-inch intervals beginning at zero and also draw a parallel line down its length, ¼ inch from the edge.
8 Make ten identical hooks out of small paper clips.
1 Put a twelve-inch ruler on a piece of cardboard.
9 Hang a paper clip from each of the ten holes.
6 Push a nail through the center line ½ inch above the intersecting line.
3 Cut the shape out of cardboard with heavy-duty scissors.
7 Rest the nail between two items of equal height such as glasses, empty cans, or books.

Number the pictures below to show the same order as above.

2 5 6 4 7
1 8 3 10 9

Try making a balance scale. If you do the above steps in order, it should work.

• Circle the largest measurement.

1 cup 4 tablespoons (1 pint) 1 ounce

Page 16

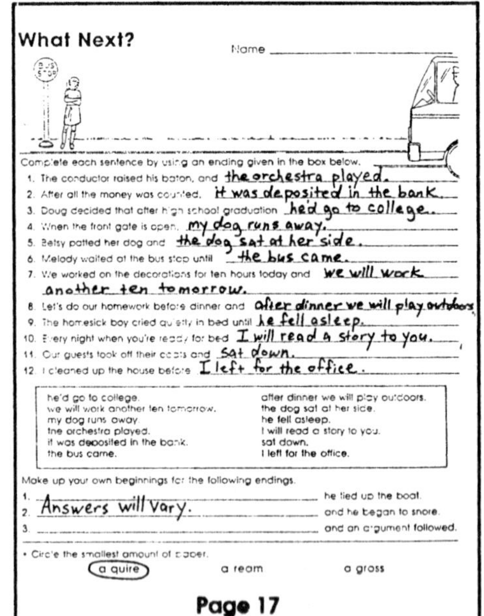

What Next?

Name

Complete each sentence by using an ending given in the box below.

1. The conductor raised his baton, and *the orchestra played.*
2. After all the money was counted, *it was deposited in the bank.*
3. Doug decided that after high school graduation *he'd go to college.*
4. When the front gate is open, *my dog runs away.*
5. Betsy patted her dog and *the dog sat at her side.*
6. Melody waited at the bus stop until *the bus came.*
7. We worked on the decorations for ten hours today and *we will work another ten tomorrow.*
8. Let's do our homework before dinner and *after dinner we will play outdoors.*
9. The homesick boy cried quietly in bed until *he fell asleep.*
10. Every night when you're ready for bed *I will read a story to you.*
11. Our guests took off their coats and *sat down.*
12. I cleaned up the house before *I left for the office.*

he'd go to college.	after dinner we will play outdoors.
we will work another ten tomorrow.	the dog sat at her side.
my dog runs away.	he fell asleep.
the orchestra played.	I will read a story to you.
it was deposited in the bank.	sat down.
the bus came.	I left for the office.

Make up your own beginnings for the following endings.

1. ______ he tied up the boat.
2. *Answers will vary.* ______ and he began to snore.
3. ______ and an argument followed.

• Circle the smallest amount of paper.

(a quire) a ream a gross

Page 17

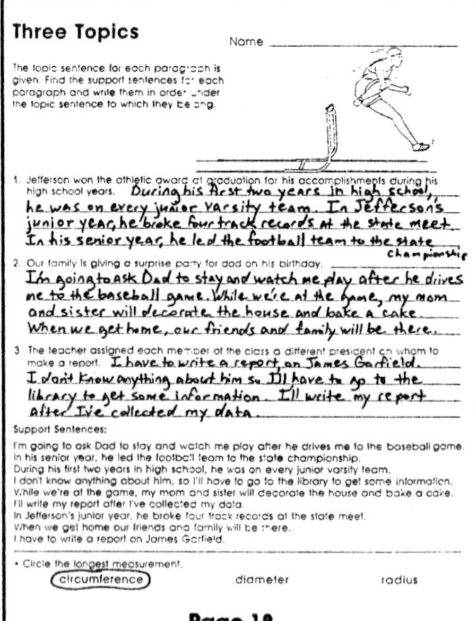

Three Topics

Name

The topic sentence for each paragraph is given. Find the support sentences for each paragraph and write them in order under the topic sentence to which they belong.

1. Jefferson won the athletic award at graduation for his accomplishments during his high school years. *During his first two years in high school, he was on every junior varsity team. In Jefferson's junior year, he broke four track records at the state meet. In his senior year, he led the football team to the state championship.*
2. Our family is giving a surprise party for dad on his birthday. *I'm going to ask Dad to stay and watch me play after he drives me to the baseball game. While we're at the game, my mom and sister will decorate the house and bake a cake. When we get home, our friends and family will be there.*
3. The teacher assigned each member of the class a different president on whom to make a report. *I have to write a report on James Garfield. I don't know anything about him so I'll have to go to the library to get some information. I'll write my report after I've collected my data.*

Support Sentences:

I'm going to ask Dad to stay and watch me play after he drives me to the baseball game.
In his senior year, he led the football team to the state championship.
During his first two years in high school, he was on every junior varsity team.
I don't know anything about him, so I'll have to go to the library to get some information.
While we're at the game, my mom and sister will decorate the house and bake a cake.
I'll write my report after I've collected my data.
In Jefferson's junior year, he broke four track records at the state meet.
When we get home our friends and family will be there.
I have to write a report on James Garfield.

• Circle the longest measurement.

(circumference) diameter radius

Page 18

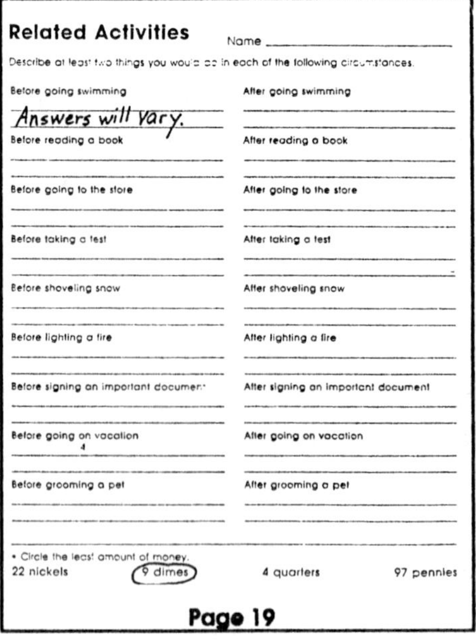

Related Activities

Name

Describe at least two things you would do in each of the following circumstances.

Before going swimming *Answers will vary.*	After going swimming
Before reading a book	After reading a book
Before going to the store	After going to the store
Before taking a test	After taking a test
Before shoveling snow	After shoveling snow
Before lighting a fire	After lighting a fire
Before signing an important document	After signing an important document
Before going on vacation	After going on vacation
Before grooming a pet	After grooming a pet

• Circle the least amount of money.

22 nickels (9 dimes) 4 quarters 97 pennies

Page 19

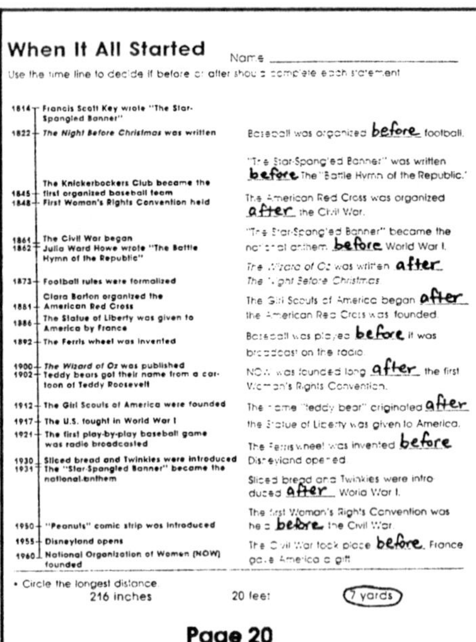

When It All Started

Name

Use the time line to decide if before or after should complete each statement.

1814 Francis Scott Key wrote "The Star-Spangled Banner"
1822 The Night Before Christmas was written
1845 The Knickerbockers Club became the first organized baseball team
1848 First Woman's Rights Convention held
1861 The Civil War began
1862 Julia Ward Howe wrote "The Battle Hymn of the Republic"
1873 Football rules were formalized
1881 Clara Barton organized the American Red Cross
1886 The Statue of Liberty was given to America by France
1892 The Ferris wheel was invented
1900 The Wizard of Oz was published
1902 Teddy bears got their name from a cartoon of Teddy Roosevelt
1912 The Girl Scouts of America were founded
1917 The U.S. fought in World War I
1921 The first play-by-play baseball game was radio broadcasted
1930 Sliced bread and Twinkies were introduced
1931 The "Star-Spangled Banner" became the national anthem
1950 "Peanuts" comic strip was introduced
1955 Disneyland opens
1960 National Organization of Women (NOW) founded

Baseball was organized *before* football.
"The Star-Spangled Banner" was written *before* the "Battle Hymn of the Republic."
The American Red Cross was organized *after* the Civil War.
"The Star-Spangled Banner" became the national anthem *before* World War I.
The Wizard of Oz was written *after* *The Night Before Christmas*.
The Girl Scouts of America began *after* the American Red Cross was founded.
Baseball was played *before* it was broadcast on the radio.
NOW was founded long *after* the first Woman's Rights Convention.
The name "teddy bear" originated *after* the Statue of Liberty was given to America.
The Ferris wheel was invented *before* Disneyland opened.
Sliced bread and Twinkies were introduced *after* World War I.
The first Woman's Rights Convention was held *before* the Civil War.
The Civil War took place *before* France gave America a gift.

• Circle the longest distance.

216 inches 20 feet (7 yards)

Page 20

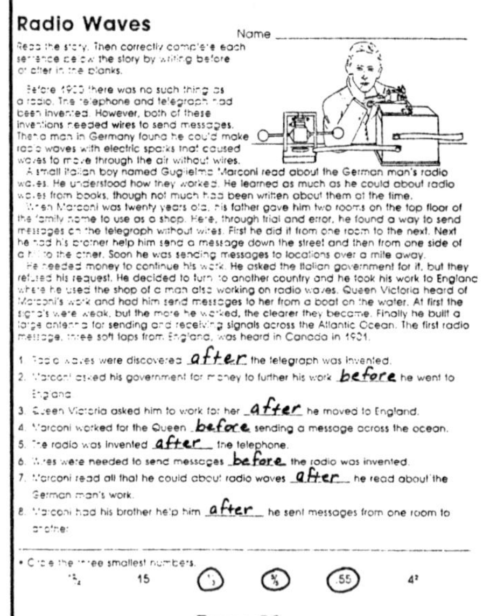

Radio Waves

Name

Read the story. Then correctly complete each sentence below the story by writing before or after in the blanks.

Before 1900 there was no such thing as a radio. The telephone and telegraph had been invented. However, both of these inventions needed wires to send messages. Then a man in Germany found he could make radio waves with electric sparks that caused waves to move through the air without wires.

A small Italian boy named Guglielmo Marconi read about the German man's radio waves. He understood how they worked. He learned as much as he could about radio waves from books, though not much had been written about them at the time.

When Marconi was twenty years old, his father gave him two rooms on the top floor of the family home to use as a shop. Here, through trial and error, he found a way to send messages on the telegraph without wires. First he did it from one room to the next. Next he had his brother help him send a message down the street and then from one side of a hill to the other. Soon he was sending messages to locations over a mile away.

He needed money to continue his work. He asked the Italian government for it, but they refused his request. He decided to turn to another country and he took his work to England where he used the shop of a man also working on radio waves. Queen Victoria heard of Marconi's work and had him send messages to her from a boat on the water. At first the signals were weak, but the more he worked, the clearer they became. Finally he built a large antenna for sending and receiving signals across the Atlantic Ocean. The first radio message, three soft taps from England, was heard in Canada in 1901.

1. Radio waves were discovered *after* the telegraph was invented.
2. Marconi asked his government for money to further his work *before* he went to England.
3. Queen Victoria asked him to work for her *after* he moved to England.
4. Marconi worked for the Queen *before* sending a message across the ocean.
5. The radio was invented *after* the telephone.
6. Wires were needed to send messages *before* the radio was invented.
7. Marconi read all that he could about radio waves *after* he read about the German man's work.
8. Marconi had his brother help him *after* he sent messages from one room to another.

• Circle the three smallest numbers.

$^{15}/_{4}$ 15 (3) ($^{6}/_{3}$) (.55) 4^{2}

Page 21

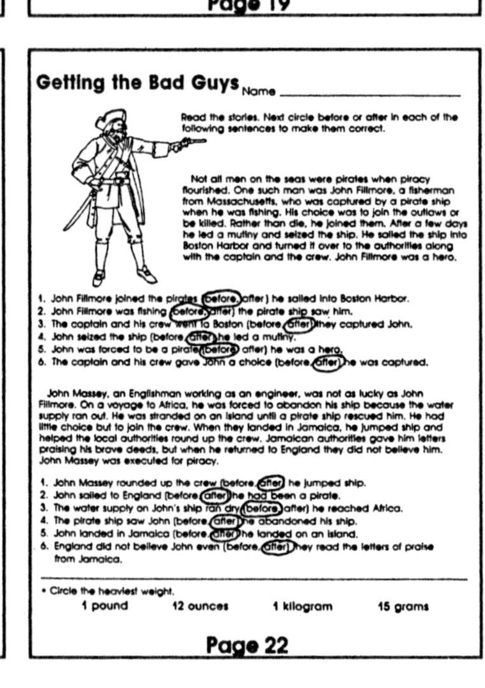

Getting the Bad Guys

Name

Read the stories. Next circle before or after in each of the following sentences to make them correct.

Not all men on the seas were pirates when piracy flourished. One such man was John Fillmore, a fisherman from Massachusetts, who was captured by a pirate ship when he was fishing. His choice was to join the outlaws or be killed. Rather than die, he joined them. After a few days he led a mutiny and seized the ship. He sailed the ship into Boston Harbor and turned it over to the authorities along with the captain and the crew. John Fillmore was a hero.

1. John Fillmore joined the pirates (before, after) he sailed into Boston Harbor. — *before*
2. John Fillmore was fishing (before, after) the pirate ship saw him. — *before*
3. The captain and his crew went to Boston (before, after) they captured John. — *after*
4. John seized the ship (before, after) he led a mutiny. — *after*
5. John was forced to be a pirate (before, after) he was a hero. — *before*
6. The captain and his crew gave John a choice (before, after) he was captured. — *after*

John Massey, an Englishman working as an engineer, was not as lucky as John Fillmore. On a voyage to Africa, he was forced to abandon his ship because the water supply ran out. He was stranded on an island until a pirate ship rescued him. He had little choice but to join the crew. When they landed in Jamaica, he jumped ship and helped the local authorities round up the pirate crew. Jamaican authorities gave him letters praising his brave deeds, but when he returned to England they did not believe him. John Massey was executed for piracy.

1. John Massey rounded up the crew (before, after) he jumped ship. — *after*
2. John sailed to England (before, after) he had been a pirate. — *after*
3. The water supply on John's ship ran dry (before, after) he reached Africa. — *before*
4. The pirate ship saw John (before, after) he abandoned his ship. — *after*
5. John landed in Jamaica (before, after) he landed on an island. — *after*
6. England did not believe John even (before, after) they read the letters of praise from Jamaica. — *after*

• Circle the heaviest weight.

1 pound 12 ounces 1 kilogram 15 grams

Page 22

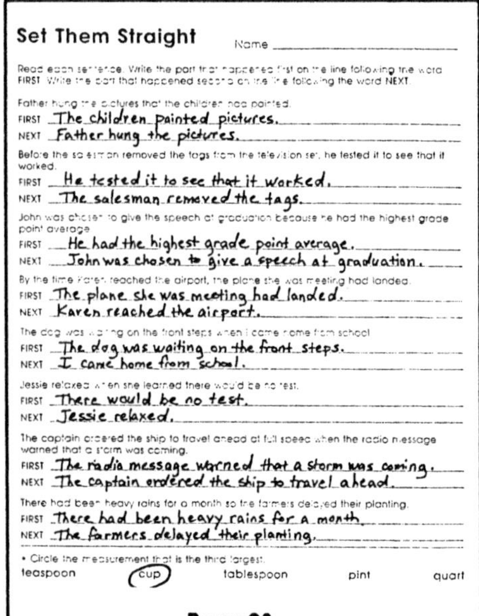

Set Them Straight

Name

Read each sentence. Write the part that happened first on the line following the word FIRST. Write the part that happened second on the line following the word NEXT.

Father hung the pictures that the children had painted.
FIRST *The children painted pictures.*
NEXT *Father hung the pictures.*

Before the salesman removed the tags from the television set, he tested it to see that it worked.
FIRST *He tested it to see that it worked.*
NEXT *The salesman removed the tags.*

John was chosen to give the speech at graduation because he had the highest grade point average.
FIRST *He had the highest grade point average.*
NEXT *John was chosen to give a speech at graduation.*

By the time Karen reached the airport, the plane she was meeting had landed.
FIRST *The plane she was meeting had landed.*
NEXT *Karen reached the airport.*

The dog was waiting on the front steps when I came home from school.
FIRST *The dog was waiting on the front steps.*
NEXT *I came home from school.*

Jessie relaxed when she learned there would be no test.
FIRST *There would be no test.*
NEXT *Jessie relaxed.*

The captain ordered the ship to travel ahead at full speed when the radio message warned that a storm was coming.
FIRST *The radio message warned that a storm was coming.*
NEXT *The captain ordered the ship to travel ahead.*

There had been heavy rains for a month so the farmers delayed their planting.
FIRST *There had been heavy rains for a month.*
NEXT *The farmers delayed their planting.*

• Circle the measurement that is the third largest.

teaspoon (cup) tablespoon pint quart

Page 23

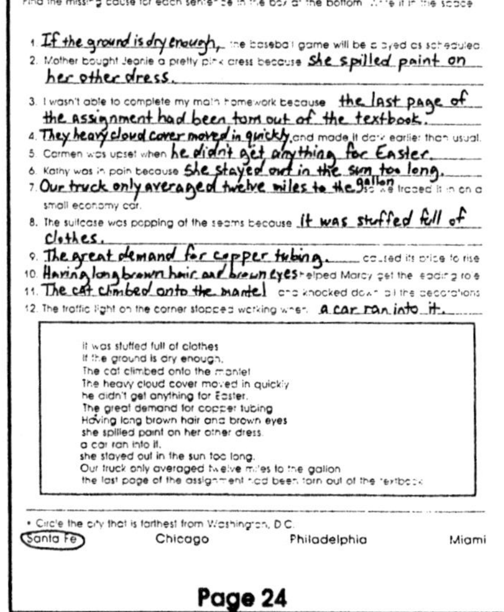

The Missing Causes

Name

Find the missing cause for each sentence in the box at the bottom. Write it in the space.

1. *If the ground is dry enough,* the baseball game will be played as scheduled.
2. Mother bought Jeanie a pretty pink dress because *she spilled paint on her other dress.*
3. I wasn't able to complete my main homework because *the last page of the assignment had been torn out of the textbook.*
4. *The heavy cloud cover moved in quickly* and made it dark earlier than usual.
5. Carmen was upset when *he didn't get anything for Easter.*
6. Kathy was in pain because *she stayed out in the sun too long.*
7. *Our truck only averaged twelve miles to the gallon* so we traded it in on a small economy car.
8. The suitcase was popping at the seams because *it was stuffed full of clothes.*
9. *The great demand for copper tubing* caused its price to rise.
10. *Having long brown hair and brown eyes* helped Marcy get the leading role.
11. *The cat climbed onto the mantel* and knocked down all the decorations.
12. The traffic light on the corner stopped working when *a car ran into it.*

it was stuffed full of clothes
if the ground is dry enough
the cat climbed onto the mantel
the heavy cloud cover moved in quickly
he didn't get anything for Easter
the great demand for copper tubing
having long brown hair and brown eyes
she spilled paint on her other dress
a car ran into it
she stayed out in the sun too long
our truck only averaged twelve miles to the gallon
the last page of the assignment had been torn out of the textbook

• Circle the city that is farthest from Washington, D.C.

(Santa Fe) Chicago Philadelphia Miami

Page 24

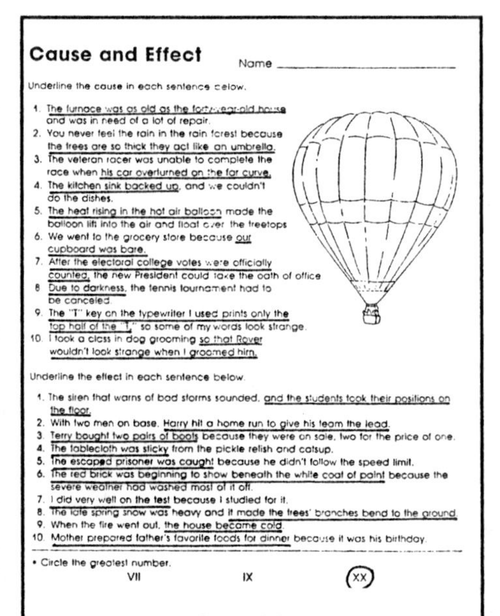

Cause and Effect

Name

Underline the cause in each sentence below.

1. The furnace was as old as the forty-year-old house and was in need of a lot of repair.
2. You never feel the rain in the rain forest because the trees are so thick they act like an umbrella.
3. The veteran racer was unable to complete the race when his car overturned on the far curve.
4. The kitchen sink backed up, and we couldn't do the dishes.
5. The heat rising in the hot air balloon made the balloon lift into the air and float over the treetops.
6. We went to the grocery store because our cupboard was bare.
7. After the electoral college votes were officially counted, the new President could take the oath of office.
8. Due to darkness, the tennis tournament had to be canceled.
9. The "T" key on the typewriter I used prints only the top half of the "T," so some of my words look strange.
10. I took a class in dog grooming so that Rover wouldn't look strange when I groomed him.

Underline the effect in each sentence below.

1. The siren that warns of bad storms sounded, and the students took their positions on the floor.
2. With two men on base, Harry hit a home run to give his team the lead.
3. Terry bought two pairs of boots because they were on sale, two for the price of one.
4. The tablecloth was sticky from the pickle relish and catsup.
5. The escaped prisoner was caught because he didn't follow the speed limit.
6. The red brick was beginning to show beneath the white coat of paint because the severe weather had washed most of it off.
7. I did very well on the test because I studied for it.
8. The late spring snow was heavy and it made the trees' branches bend to the ground.
9. When the fire went out, the house became cold.
10. Mother prepared father's favorite foods for dinner because it was his birthday.

• Circle the greatest number.

VII IX (XX)

Page 25

So What Then?

Name ______________

Match the sentence parts that go together best. Write the number of the first part on the line in front of the last part for each one.

1. If you bake the cake,
2. If you close your eyes and count to ten,
3. If the Constitution of the United States had not been written,
4. If no one is on recess duty,
5. If you don't have a raincoat,
6. If you can't sit still now,
7. If the taxi doesn't come on time,
8. If Barbara has a green blouse,
9. If there are any leftovers,
10. If I am late for dinner,
11. If the students don't have permission slips,
12. If the schedule in the newspaper is correct,
13. If you tie a string on your finger,
14. If you see a penny, pick it up
15. If you don't answer the phone,
16. If the sun shines on the furniture,
17. If the children want ice cream,
18. If the music is too loud,
19. If the wind would stop blowing,
20. If there are more than forty people on the bus,

8 she should wear it on St. Patrick's Day.
5 I'll lend you one to wear during the storm.
11 they can't go on the field trip.
3 state governments might be responsible only to themselves
14 and all the day you'll have good luck.
16 put down the awnings.
1 I'll make the icing.
6 you'll never be able to sit through the three-hour show.
13 it will help you remember.
2 you will be surprised at what you see when you open your eyes.
7 our neighbor will take us to the airport.
4 there will be many more accidents.
10 I will eat it cold.
17 they'll have to finish their meal.
18 move away from the speakers
20 you will have to wait for the next one.
9 give them to the dog.
15 I'll know you went without me.
19 I'd go out for a walk.
12 the town meeting begins at 7:00 p.m.

• Which one shows 108? Circle it.

Page 26

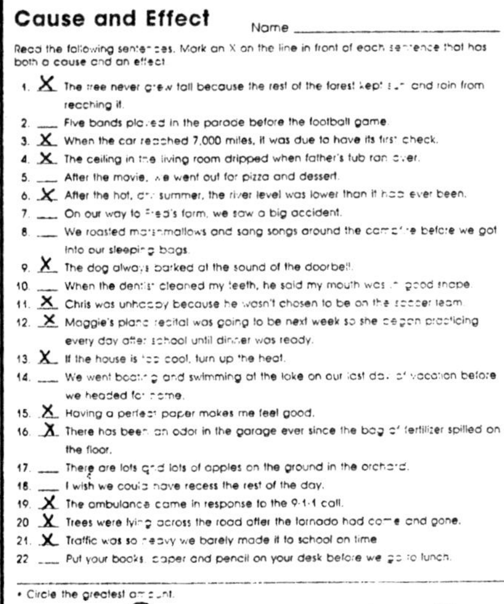

Cause and Effect

Name ______________

Read the following sentences. Mark an X on the line in front of each sentence that has both a cause and an effect.

1. X The tree never grew tall because the rest of the forest kept sun and rain from reaching it.
2. ___ Five bands played in the parade before the football game.
3. X When the car reached 7,000 miles, it was due to have its first check.
4. X The ceiling in the living room dripped when father's tub ran over.
5. ___ After the movie, we went out for pizza and dessert.
6. X After the hot, dry summer, the river level was lower than it had ever been.
7. ___ On our way to Fred's farm, we saw a big accident.
8. ___ We roasted marshmallows and sang songs around the campfire before we got into our sleeping bags.
9. X The dog always barked at the sound of the doorbell.
10. ___ When the dentist cleaned my teeth, he said my mouth was in good shape.
11. X Chris was unhappy because he wasn't chosen to be on the soccer team.
12. X Maggie's piano recital was going to be next week so she began practicing every day after school until dinner was ready.
13. X If the house is too cool, turn up the heat.
14. ___ We went boating and swimming at the lake on our last day of vacation before we headed for home.
15. X Having a perfect paper makes me feel good.
16. X There has been an odor in the garage ever since the bag of fertilizer spilled on the floor.
17. ___ There are lots and lots of apples on the ground in the orchard.
18. ___ I wish we could have recess the rest of the day.
19. X The ambulance came in response to the 9-1-1 call.
20. X Trees were lying across the road after the tornado had come and gone.
21. X Traffic was so heavy we barely made it to school on time.
22. ___ Put your books, paper and pencil on your desk before we go to lunch.

• Circle the greatest amount.

.1 (.5) .01 .05 .005 .001

Page 27

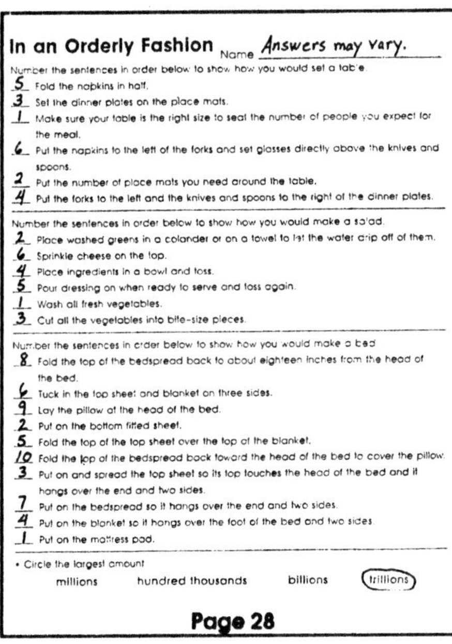

In an Orderly Fashion

Name *Answers may vary.*

Number the sentences in order below to show how you would set a table.

5 Fold the napkins in half.
3 Set the dinner plates on the place mats.
1 Make sure your table is the right size to seat the number of people you expect for the meal.
6 Put the napkins to the left of the forks and set glasses directly above the knives and spoons.
2 Put the number of place mats you need around the table.
4 Put the forks to the left and the knives and spoons to the right of the dinner plates.

Number the sentences in order below to show how you would make a salad.

2 Place washed greens in a colander or on a towel to let the water drip off of them.
6 Sprinkle cheese on the top.
4 Place ingredients in a bowl and toss.
5 Pour dressing on when ready to serve and toss again.
1 Wash all fresh vegetables.
3 Cut all the vegetables into bite-size pieces.

Number the sentences in order below to show how you would make a bed.

8 Fold the top of the bedspread back to about eighteen inches from the head of the bed.
6 Tuck in the top sheet and blanket on three sides.
9 Lay the pillow at the head of the bed.
2 Put on the bottom fitted sheet.
5 Fold the top of the top sheet over the top of the blanket.
10 Fold the top of the bedspread back toward the head of the bed to cover the pillow.
3 Put on and spread the top sheet so its top touches the head of the bed and it hangs over the end and two sides.
7 Put on the bedspread so it hangs over the end and two sides.
4 Put on the blanket so it hangs over the foot of the bed and two sides.
1 Put on the mattress pad.

• Circle the largest amount.

millions hundred thousands billions (trillions)

Page 28

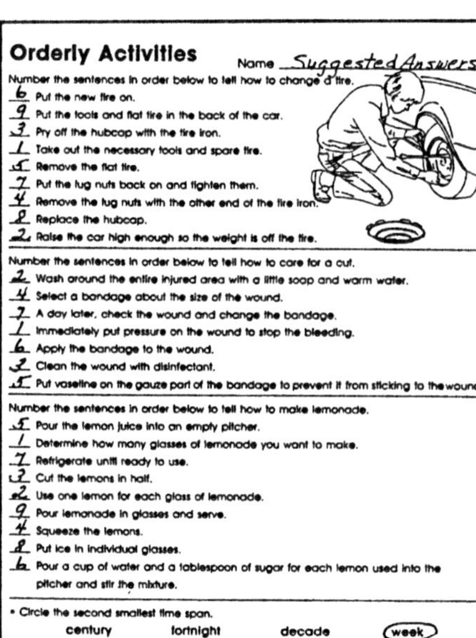

Orderly Activities

Name *Suggested Answers*

Number the sentences in order below to tell how to change a tire.

6 Put the new tire on.
9 Put the tools and flat tire in the back of the car.
3 Pry off the hubcap with the tire iron.
1 Take out the necessary tools and spare tire.
5 Remove the flat tire.
7 Put the lug nuts back on and tighten them.
4 Remove the lug nuts with the other end of the tire iron.
8 Replace the hubcap.
2 Raise the car high enough so the weight is off the tire.

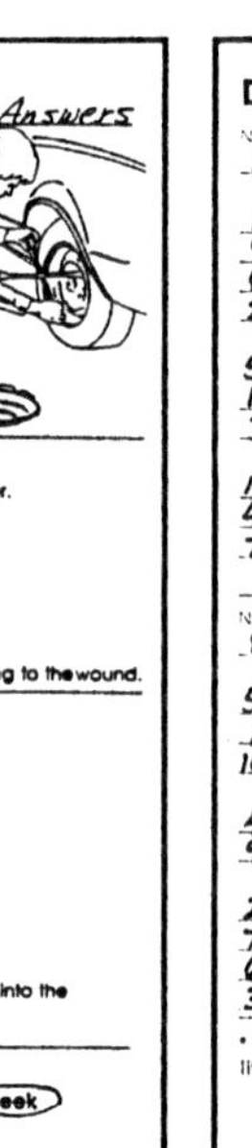

Number the sentences in order below to tell how to care for a cut.

2 Wash around the entire injured area with a little soap and warm water.
4 Select a bandage about the size of the wound.
7 A day later, check the wound and change the bandage.
1 Immediately put pressure on the wound to stop the bleeding.
6 Apply the bandage to the wound.
3 Clean the wound with disinfectant.
5 Put vaseline on the gauze part of the bandage to prevent it from sticking to the wound.

Number the sentences in order below to tell how to make lemonade.

5 Pour the lemon juice into an empty pitcher.
1 Determine how many glasses of lemonade you want to make.
7 Refrigerate until ready to use.
3 Cut the lemons in half.
2 Use one lemon for each glass of lemonade.
9 Pour lemonade in glasses and serve.
4 Squeeze the lemons.
8 Put ice in individual glasses.
6 Pour a cup of water and a tablespoon of sugar for each lemon used into the pitcher and stir the mixture.

• Circle the second smallest time span.

century fortnight decade (week)

Page 29

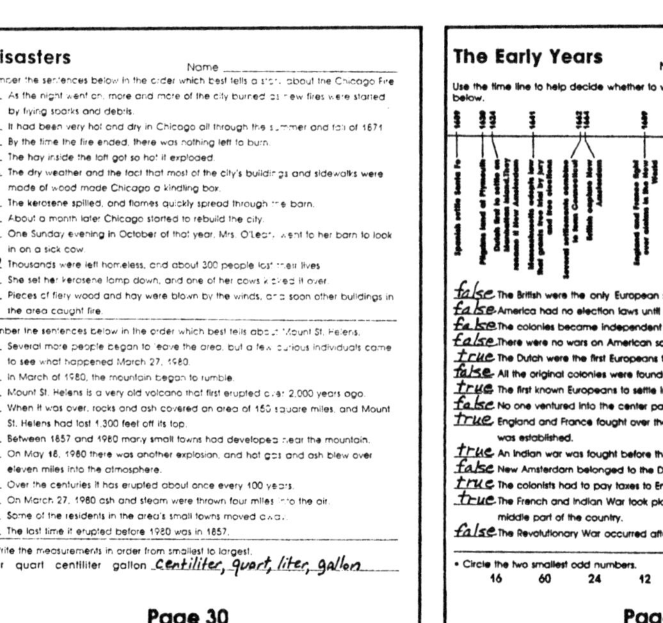

Disasters

Name ______________

Number the sentences below in the order which best tells a story about the Chicago Fire.

8 As the night went on, more and more of the city burned as new fires were started by flying sparks and debris.
1 It had been very hot and dry in Chicago all through the summer and fall of 1871.
9 By the time the fire ended, there was nothing left to burn.
6 The hay inside the loft got so hot it exploded.
2 The dry weather and the fact that most of the city's buildings and sidewalks were made of wood made Chicago a kindling box.
5 The kerosene spilled, and flames quickly spread through the barn.
11 About a month later Chicago started to rebuild the city.
3 One Sunday evening in October of that year, Mrs. O'Leary went to her barn to look in on a sick cow.
10 Thousands were left homeless, and about 300 people lost their lives.
4 She set her kerosene lamp down, and one of her cows kicked it over.
7 Pieces of fiery wood and hay were blown by the winds, and soon other buildings in the area caught fire.

Number the sentences below in the order which best tells about Mount St. Helens.

8 Several more people began to leave the area, but a few curious individuals came to see what happened March 27, 1980.
5 In March of 1980, the mountain began to rumble.
1 Mount St. Helens is a very old volcano that first erupted over 2,000 years ago.
10 When it was over, rocks and ash covered an area of 150 square miles, and Mount St. Helens had lost 1,300 feet off its top.
4 Between 1857 and 1980 many small towns had developed near the mountain.
9 On May 18, 1980 there was another explosion, and hot gas and ash blew over eleven miles into the atmosphere.
2 Over the centuries it has erupted about once every 100 years.
7 On March 27, 1980 ash and steam were thrown four miles into the air.
6 Some of the residents in the area's small towns moved away.
3 The last time it erupted before 1980 was in 1857.

• Write the measurements in order from smallest to largest.

liter quart centiliter gallon *centiliter, quart, liter, gallon*

Page 30

The Early Years

Name ______________

Use the time line to help decide whether to write true or false before each statement below.

false The British were the only European settlers in America.
false America had no election laws until the Constitution was written.
false The colonies became independent before the Revolutionary War began.
false There were no wars on American soil until the Revolution.
true The Dutch were the first Europeans to settle New Amsterdam.
false All the original colonies were founded before the French and Indian Wars.
true The first known Europeans to settle in Massachusetts were the Pilgrims.
false No one ventured into the center part of the country until after the Revolution.
true England and France fought over their claims in America before the last colony was established.
true An Indian war was fought before the Revolution.
false New Amsterdam belonged to the Dutch after 1664.
true The colonists had to pay taxes to England before the Revolutionary War.
true The French and Indian War took place before Daniel Boone explored the middle part of the country.
false The Revolutionary War occurred after the Constitution was written.

• Circle the two smallest odd numbers.

16 60 24 12 (9) 36 45 (25)

Page 31

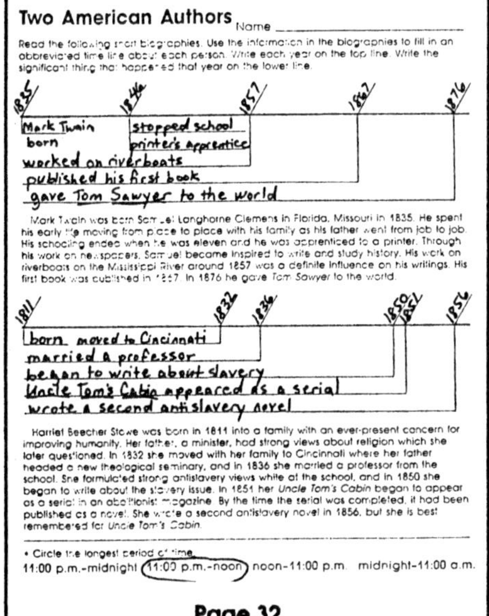

Two American Authors

Name ______________

Read the following short biographies. Use the information in the biographies to fill in an abbreviated time line about each person. Write each year on the top line. Write the significant thing that happened that year on the lower line.

1835 Mark Twain born
1846 stopped school, printer's apprentice
1857 worked on riverboats
1867 published his first book
1876 gave Tom Sawyer to the world

Mark Twain was born Samuel Langhorne Clemens in Florida, Missouri in 1835. He spent his early life moving from place to place with his family as his father went from job to job. His schooling ended when he was eleven and he was apprenticed to a printer. Through his work on newspapers, Samuel became inspired to write and study history. His work on riverboats on the Mississippi River around 1857 was a definite influence on his writings. His first book was published in 1867. In 1876 he gave *Tom Sawyer* to the world.

1811 born
1832 moved to Cincinnati
1836 married a professor
1850 began to write about slavery
1851 Uncle Tom's Cabin appeared as a serial
1856 wrote a second antislavery novel

Harriet Beecher Stowe was born in 1811 into a family with an ever-present concern for improving humanity. Her father, a minister, had strong views about religion which she later questioned. In 1832 she moved with her family to Cincinnati where her father headed a new theological seminary, and in 1836 she married a professor from the school. She formulated strong antislavery views while at the school, and in 1850 she began to write about the slavery issue. In 1851 her *Uncle Tom's Cabin* began to appear as a serial in an abolitionist magazine. By the time the serial was completed, it had been published as a novel. She wrote a second antislavery novel in 1856, but she is best remembered for *Uncle Tom's Cabin*.

• Circle the longest period of time.

11:00 p.m.-midnight (11:00 p.m.-noon) noon-11:00 p.m. midnight-11:00 a.m.

Page 32

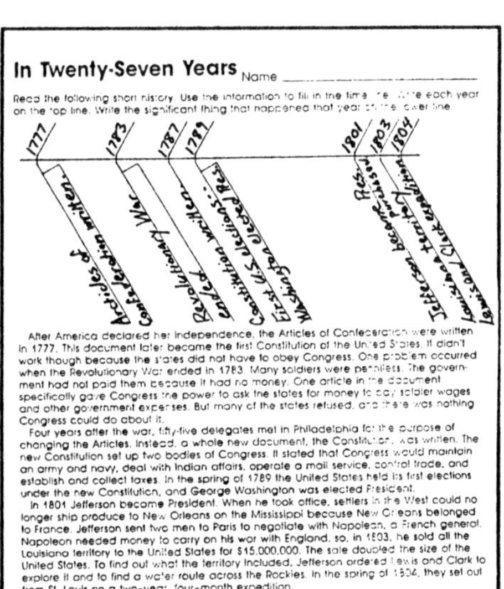

In Twenty-Seven Years

Name ______________

Read the following short history. Use the information to fill in the time line. Write each year on the top line. Write the significant thing that happened that year on the lower line.

1777 Articles of Confederation written
1783 Revolutionary War ended
1787 Constitution written
1789 First U.S. elections; Washington elected President
1801 Jefferson became President
1803 Louisiana Territory purchased
1804 Lewis and Clark expedition

After America declared her independence, the Articles of Confederation were written in 1777. This document later became the first Constitution of the United States. It didn't work though because the states did not have to obey Congress. One problem occurred when the Revolutionary War ended in 1783. Many soldiers were penniless. The government had not paid them because it had no money. One article in the document specifically gave Congress the power to ask the states for money to pay soldier wages and other government expenses. But many of the states refused, and there was nothing Congress could do about it.

Four years after the war, fifty-five delegates met in Philadelphia for the purpose of changing the Articles. Instead, a whole new document, the Constitution, was written. The new Constitution set up two bodies of Congress. It stated that Congress would maintain an army and navy, deal with Indian affairs, operate a mail service, control trade, and establish and collect taxes. In the spring of 1789 the United States held its first elections under the new Constitution, and George Washington was elected President.

In 1801 Jefferson became President. When he took office, settlers in the West could no longer ship produce to New Orleans on the Mississippi because New Orleans belonged to France. Jefferson sent two men to Paris to negotiate with Napoleon, a French general. Napoleon needed money to carry on his war with England, so, in 1803, he sold all the Louisiana territory to the United States for $15,000,000. The sale doubled the size of the United States. To find out what the territory included, Jefferson ordered Lewis and Clark to explore it and to find a water route across the Rockies. In the spring of 1804, they set out from St. Louis on a two-year, four-month expedition.

• Circle the shape that has the least number of sides.

octagon hexagon (pentagon)

Page 33

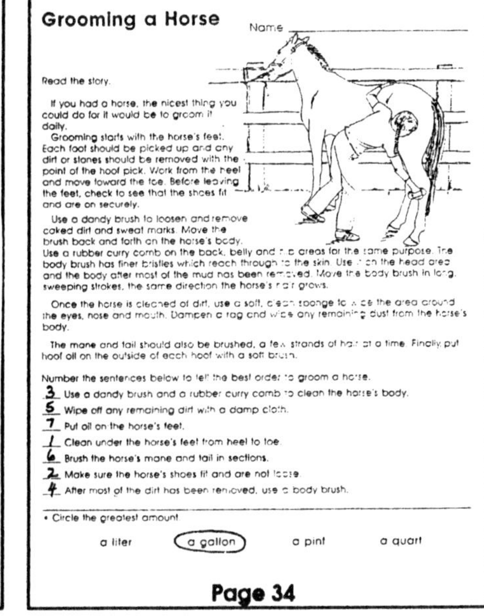

Grooming a Horse

Name ______________

Read the story.

If you had a horse, the nicest thing you could do for it would be to groom it daily.

Grooming starts with the horse's feet. Each foot should be picked up and any dirt or stones should be removed with the point of the hoof pick. Work from the heel and move toward the toe. Before leaving the feet, check to see that the shoes fit and are on securely.

Use a dandy brush to loosen and remove caked dirt and sweat marks. Move the brush back and forth on the horse's body. Use a rubber curry comb on the back, belly and hip areas for the same purpose. The body brush has finer bristles which reach through to the skin. Use it on the head area and the body after most of the mud has been removed. Move the body brush in long, sweeping strokes, the same direction the horse's hair grows.

Once the horse is cleaned of dirt, use a soft, clean sponge to wipe the area around the eyes, nose and mouth. Dampen a rag and wipe any remaining dust from the horse's body.

The mane and tail should also be brushed, a few strands of hair at a time. Finally, put hoof oil on the outside of each hoof with a soft brush.

Number the sentences below to tell the best order to groom a horse.

3 Use a dandy brush and a rubber curry comb to clean the horse's body.
5 Wipe off any remaining dirt with a damp cloth.
7 Put oil on the horse's feet.
1 Clean under the horse's feet from heel to toe.
6 Brush the horse's mane and tail in sections.
2 Make sure the horse's shoes fit and are not loose.
4 After most of the dirt has been removed, use a body brush.

• Circle the greatest amount.

a liter (a gallon) a pint a quart

Page 34

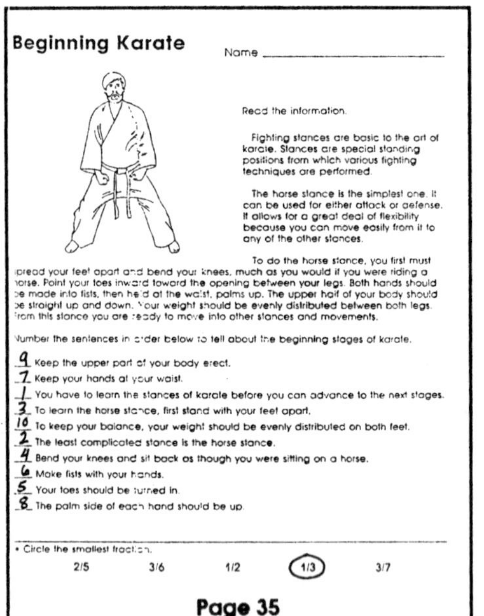

Beginning Karate

Name ____________

Read the information.

Fighting stances are basic to the art of karate. Stances are special standing positions from which various fighting techniques are performed.

The horse stance is the simplest one. It can be used for either attack or defense. It allows for a great deal of flexibility because you can move easily from it to any of the other stances.

To do the horse stance, you first must spread your feet apart and bend your knees, much as you would if you were riding a horse. Point your toes inward toward the opening between your legs. Both hands should be made into fists, then held at the waist, palms up. The upper half of your body should be straight up and down. Your weight should be evenly distributed between both legs. From this stance you are ready to move into other stances and movements.

Number the sentences in order below to tell about the beginning stages of karate.

9 Keep the upper part of your body erect.
7 Keep your hands at your waist.
1 You have to learn the stances of karate before you can advance to the next stages.
3 To learn the horse stance, first stand with your feet apart.
10 To keep your balance, your weight should be evenly distributed on both feet.
2 The least complicated stance is the horse stance.
4 Bend your knees and sit back as though you were sitting on a horse.
6 Make fists with your hands.
5 Your toes should be turned in.
8 The palm side of each hand should be up.

• Circle the smallest fraction.
2/5 3/6 1/2 (1/3) 3/7

Page 35

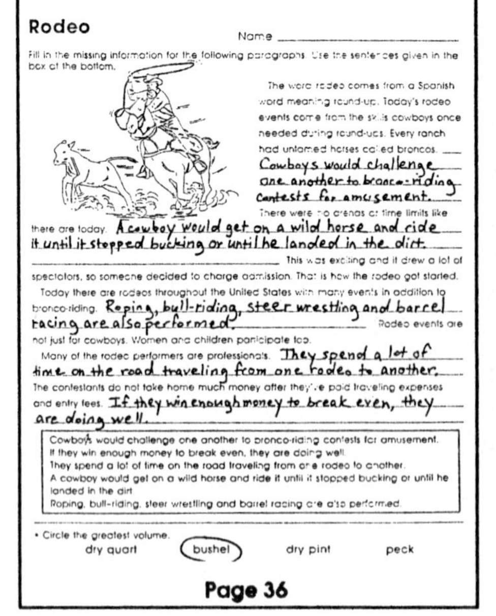

Rodeo

Name ____________

Fill in the missing information for the following paragraphs. Use the sentences given in the box at the bottom.

The word rodeo comes from a Spanish word meaning round-up. Today's rodeo events come from the skills cowboys once needed during round-ups. Every ranch had untamed horses called broncos. Cowboys would challenge one another to bronco-riding contests for amusement. There were no arenas or time limits like there are today. A cowboy would get on a wild horse and ride it until it stopped bucking or until he landed in the dirt. This was exciting and it drew a lot of spectators, so someone decided to charge admission. That is how the rodeo got started.

Today there are rodeos throughout the United States with many events in addition to bronco-riding. Roping, bull-riding, steer wrestling and barrel racing are also performed. Rodeo events are not just for cowboys. Women and children participate too.

Many of the rodeo performers are professionals. They spend a lot of time on the road traveling from one rodeo to another. The contestants do not take home much money after they've paid traveling expenses and entry fees. If they win enough money to break even, they are doing well.

Cowboys would challenge one another to bronco-riding contests for amusement.
If they win enough money to break even, they are doing well.
They spend a lot of time on the road traveling from one rodeo to another.
A cowboy would get on a wild horse and ride it until it stopped bucking or until he landed in the dirt.
Roping, bull-riding, steer wrestling and barrel racing are also performed.

• Circle the greatest volume.
dry quart (bushel) dry pint peck

Page 36

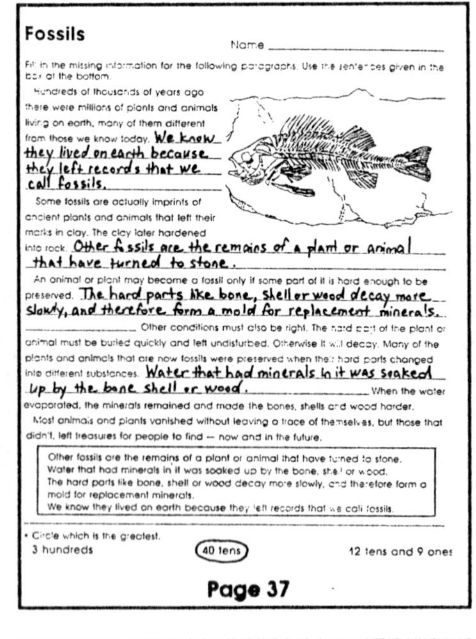

Fossils

Name ____________

Fill in the missing information for the following paragraphs. Use the sentences given in the box at the bottom.

Hundreds of thousands of years ago there were millions of plants and animals living on earth, many of them different from those we know today. We know they lived on earth because they left records that we call fossils.

Some fossils are actually imprints of ancient plants and animals that left their marks in clay. The clay later hardened into rock. Other fossils are the remains of a plant or animal that have turned to stone.

An animal or plant may become a fossil only if some part of it is hard enough to be preserved. The hard parts like bone, shell or wood decay more slowly, and therefore form a mold for replacement minerals. Other conditions must also be right. The hard part of the plant or animal must be buried quickly and left undisturbed. Otherwise it will decay. Many of the plants and animals that are now fossils were preserved when their hard parts changed into different substances. Water that had minerals in it was soaked up by the bone, shell or wood. When the water evaporated, the minerals remained and made the bones, shells and wood harder.

Most animals and plants vanished without leaving a trace of themselves, but those that didn't, left treasures for people to find — now and in the future.

Other fossils are the remains of a plant or animal that have turned to stone.
Water that had minerals in it was soaked up by the bone, shell or wood.
The hard parts like bone, shell or wood decay more slowly, and therefore form a mold for replacement minerals.
We know they lived on earth because they left records that we call fossils.

• Circle which is the greatest.
3 hundreds (40 tens) 12 tens and 9 ones

Page 37

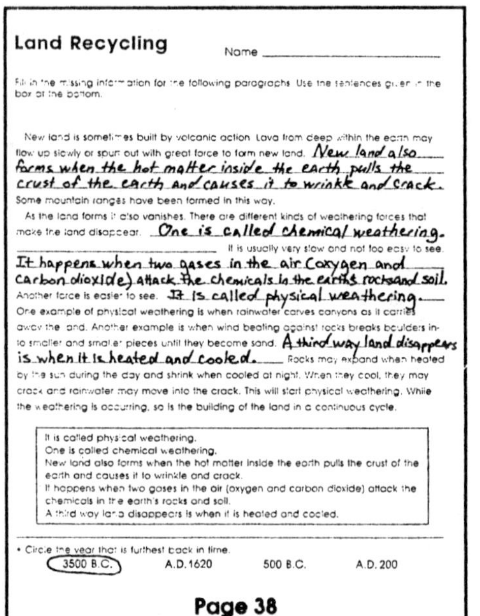

Land Recycling

Name ____________

Fill in the missing information for the following paragraphs. Use the sentences given in the box at the bottom.

New land is sometimes built by volcanic action. Lava from deep within the earth may flow up slowly or spurt out with great force to form new land. New land also forms when the hot matter inside the earth pulls the crust of the earth and causes it to wrinkle and crack. Some mountain ranges have been formed in this way.

As the land forms it also vanishes. There are different kinds of weathering forces that make the land disappear. One is called chemical weathering. It is usually very slow and not too easy to see. It happens when two gases in the air (oxygen and carbon dioxide) attack the chemicals in the earth's rocks and soil. Another force is easier to see. It is called physical weathering. One example of physical weathering is when rainwater carves canyons as it carries away the land. Another example is when wind beating against rocks breaks boulders into smaller and smaller pieces until they become sand. A third way land disappears is when it is heated and cooled. Rocks may expand when heated by the sun during the day and shrink when cooled at night. When they cool, they may crack and rainwater may move into the crack. This will start physical weathering. While the weathering is occurring, so is the building of the land in a continuous cycle.

It is called physical weathering.
One is called chemical weathering.
New land also forms when the hot matter inside the earth pulls the crust of the earth and causes it to wrinkle and crack.
It happens when two gases in the air (oxygen and carbon dioxide) attack the chemicals in the earth's rocks and soil.
A third way land disappears is when it is heated and cooled.

• Circle the year that is furthest back in time.
(3500 B.C.) A.D.1620 500 B.C. A.D.200

Page 38

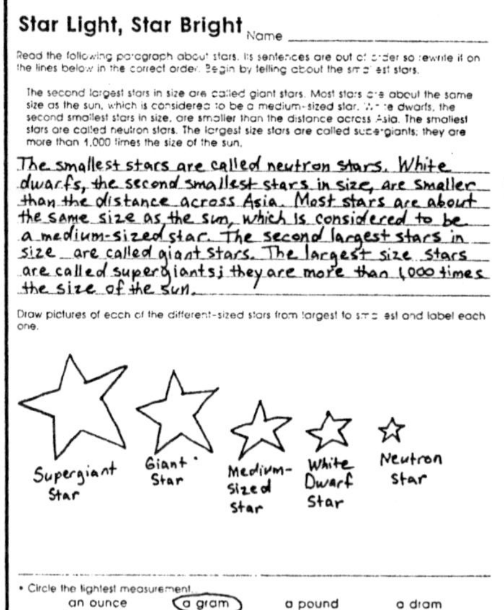

Star Light, Star Bright

Name ____________

Read the following paragraph about stars. Its sentences are out of order so rewrite it on the lines below in the correct order. Begin by telling about the smallest stars.

The second largest stars in size are called giant stars. Most stars are about the same size as the sun, which is considered to be a medium-sized star. White dwarfs, the second smallest stars in size, are smaller than the distance across Asia. The smallest stars are called neutron stars. The largest size stars are called supergiants; they are more than 1,000 times the size of the sun.

The smallest stars are called neutron stars. White dwarfs, the second smallest stars in size, are smaller than the distance across Asia. Most stars are about the same size as the sun, which is considered to be a medium-sized star. The second largest stars in size are called giant stars. The largest size stars are called supergiants; they are more than 1,000 times the size of the sun.

Draw pictures of each of the different-sized stars from largest to smallest and label each one.

Supergiant Star | Giant Star | Medium-Sized Star | White Dwarf Star | Neutron Star

• Circle the lightest measurement.
an ounce (a gram) a pound a dram

Page 39

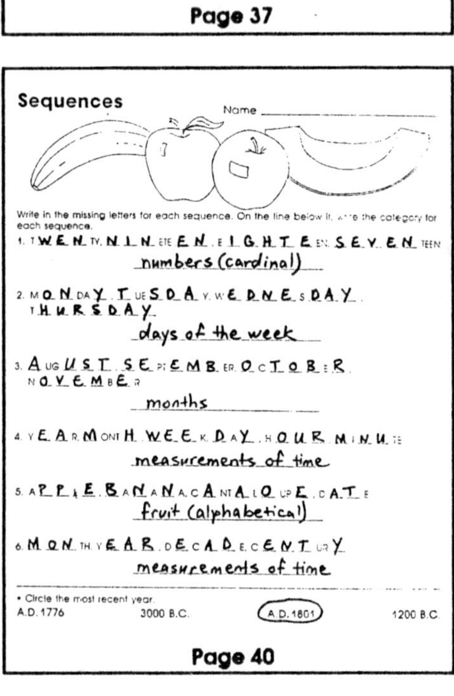

Sequences

Name ____________

Write in the missing letters for each sequence. On the line below it, write the category for each sequence.

1. TWENTY, NINETEEN, EIGHTEEN, SEVENTEEN
numbers (cardinal)
2. MONDAY, TUESDAY, WEDNESDAY, THURSDAY
days of the week
3. AUGUST, SEPTEMBER, OCTOBER, NOVEMBER
months
4. YEAR, MONTH, WEEK, DAY, HOUR, MINUTE
measurements of time
5. APPLE, BANANA, CANTALOUPE, DATE
fruit (alphabetical)
6. MONTH, YEAR, DECADE, CENTURY
measurements of time

• Circle the most recent year.
A.D.1776 3000 B.C. (A.D.1801) 1200 B.C.

Page 40

Sequence Words Suggested answers.

Name ____________

Circle the sequence word or words in each sentence.

1. The (first) thing I did when I got home was take off my shoes.
2. The guests arrived at Dan's surprise party fifteen minutes (ahead) of time.
3. It will (soon) be time for Aunt Meg and Uncle Jack to leave for the airport.
4. The boy in (front) of Bill cut in line.
5. Every (fifth) person in the lunch line got an extra cookie.
6. Father had to wait for me to pick him up because his train got in (early).
7. We can watch television (after) dinner.
8. Father waited (until) dark (before) he went fishing.
9. The (premature) baby weighed 2½ pounds.
10. The boy scout carried the flag at the (head) of the parade.
11. (Formerly) we received notices to let us know the meetings were to be held.
12. A letter was sent out by City Hall (prior) to closing off Main Street.
13. The room had (previously) been painted pink.
14. The teacher was (behind) her desk.
15. It started to rain Tuesday, and it continued for five (succeeding) days.
16. The weatherman said snow is expected (tomorrow).
17. No one has been in the attic (since) the fire.
18. Turn to the (following) page to find the answer to the riddle.
19. The letter must be mailed (immediately).
20. A vote was taken in closed session (preceding) the general convention.
21. We went on a picnic (yesterday).
22. Sally was the (second) one to complete her work.
23. The President's speech was sent to the press in (advance) of its release.
24. The doctor saw me (sooner) than he expected.
25. The award was given (posthumously) to the soldier's family.
26. Bring me the needle and thread (now) and I will sew the button on your shirt.
27. The scout troop was in the (rear) car of the train.
28. The (next) batter hit a homerun and tied the game.
29. Casey came in (last) in the contest.
30. I will call you (later) to let you know when the movie starts.

• Circle the longest measurement.
a decimeter (a meter) a foot a yard

Page 41

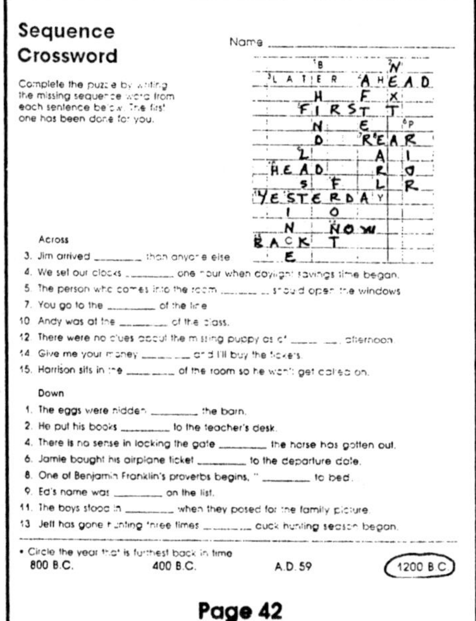

Sequence Crossword

Name ____________

Complete the puzzle by writing the missing sequence word from each sentence below. The first one has been done for you.

Across: LATER, AHEAD, FIRST, REAR, HEAD, YESTERDAY, NOW, BACK
Down: BEHIND, NEXT, FRONT, EARLY, LAST, TODAY, BEFORE

Across
3. Jim arrived ______ than anyone else.
4. We set our clocks ______ one hour when daylight savings time began.
5. The person who comes into the room ______ should open the windows.
7. You go to the ______ of the line.
10. Andy was at the ______ of the class.
12. There were no clues about the missing puppy as of ______ afternoon.
14. Give me your money ______ and I'll buy the tickets.
15. Harrison sits in the ______ of the room so he won't get called on.

Down
1. The eggs were hidden ______ the barn.
2. He put his books ______ to the teacher's desk.
4. There is no sense in locking the gate ______ the horse has gotten out.
6. Jamie bought his airplane ticket ______ to the departure date.
8. One of Benjamin Franklin's proverbs begins, "______ to bed.
9. Ed's name was ______ on the list.
11. The boys stood in ______ when they posed for the family picture.
13. Jeff has gone hunting three times ______ duck hunting season began.

• Circle the year that is furthest back in time.
800 B.C. 400 B.C. A.D.59 (1200 B.C.)

Page 42

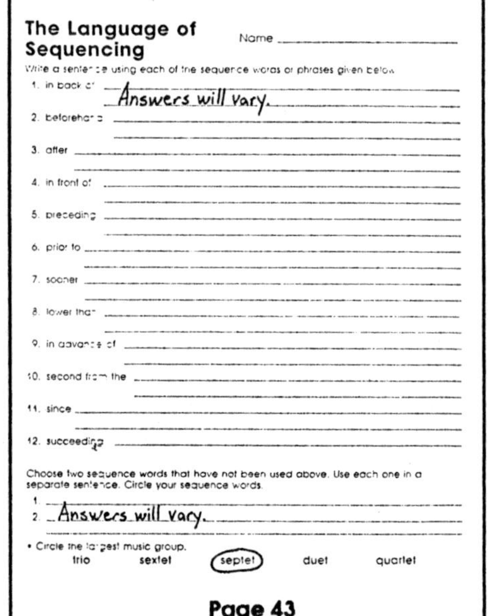

The Language of Sequencing

Name ____________

Write a sentence using each of the sequence words or phrases given below.

1. in back of — Answers will vary.
2. beforehand
3. after
4. in front of
5. preceding
6. prior to
7. sooner
8. lower than
9. in advance of
10. second from the
11. since
12. succeeding

Choose two sequence words that have not been used above. Use each one in a separate sentence. Circle your sequence words.

1.
2. Answers will vary.

• Circle the largest music group.
trio sextet (septet) duet quartet

Page 43